TABLE OF CONTENTS

INTRODUCTION

One of the most significant foreign policy dilemmas for the United States is the current stalemate with the Islamic Republic of Iran over nuclear proliferation, opposition to the existence of Israel, and state sponsorship of terrorism. A nuclear-armed Iran is likely within the next decade, a scenario many in the United States and throughout the international community consider unacceptable. The history of U.S.-Iran relations, since the Central Intelligence Agency (CIA) orchestrated coup of Iranian Prime Minister Mohammad Mossadeq in 1953, is one of mutual misunderstanding and policy miscalculation. Although successive American presidents since Iran's 1979 revolution have tried to improve relations, each effort failed because policy makers refused to apply the lessons of their predecessors and adjust the context through which they viewed Iran. The terrorist attacks of September 11, 2001, however, provided an unprecedented opportunity for a strategic rapprochement between the United States and the Islamic Republic of Iran. Few recognize that after the attacks of 9/11, Iran not only denounced the attacks but also cooperated with the United States multilaterally through the United Nations 6+2 talks on Afghanistan, and bilaterally through the Geneva Contact Group discussions on Afghanistan and Iraq. Iranian cooperation culminated in 2003 with an offer to negotiate a comprehensive resolution of differences with no preconditions, but President George W. Bush rejected this offer.

An examination of the historical context of U.S.-Iran relations since 1953, the three efforts at rapprochement since 1979, and the unprecedented nature of U.S.-Iran dialogue and cooperation after 9/11, will demonstrate how the Bush administration missed an unprecedented opportunity for rapprochement with Iran between 2001 and 2003. Part one begins with a history of Iran and a review of U.S.-Iran relations during the twentieth-century, particularly the last 60 years, in order to generate the proper context. This section concludes with an analysis of Iran's 1979 Islamic revolution and subsequent U.S. Embassy takeover in order to demonstrate the

1

opposing perspectives through which each side viewed the other during this tumultuous period. Ultimately, mutual misinterpretations of the events of 1953 and 1979 conspired to plague U.S.-Iran relations for the next three decades.

Part two examines U.S.-Iran relations from 1980 to 2000, particularly the efforts by each successive American administration to develop Iran policy and improve relations. From President Reagan's weapons for hostages scheme and President George H.W. Bush's Picco channel with Iranian President Ali Rafsanjani, to President Clinton's dual containment strategy and track-two diplomacy with Iranian President Mohammad Khatami, each effort failed primarily as a result of the lack of formal diplomatic relations. This period in U.S.-Iran relations served to demonstrate how unfamiliarity breeds contempt and distrust. For America, Iran was not a priority, and the lack of a comprehensive Iran policy only complicated matters. This section concludes with an analysis of internal Iranian politics at the turn of the century. The election of Iranian President Khatami in 1997 presented the best opportunity yet to engage Iran, but as demonstrated, this approach needed more common ground and diplomatic patience in order to succeed.

Part three focuses exclusively on the period from 2001-2003, and examines the complicated nature of Iranian cooperation with the United States after 9/11. The George W. Bush administration, without a coherent Iran policy, initially cooperated with Iran. Multilateral discussions on Afghanistan in 2001 quickly expanded into bilateral discussions and cooperation in Afghanistan and Iraq. With a post-9/11 surplus of political capital, the administration, after the successful campaign in Afghanistan and with an eye towards Iraq, began to rely on a one size fits all pre-emptive foreign policy prescribed by the new Bush Doctrine. Despite the progress of political reform in Iran, unprecedented cooperation on Afghanistan, and unconditional offers to resume normal diplomatic relations, neoconservatives within the White House and Department of Defense hijacked the foreign policy process and pursued a short-sighted policy of Iranian regime change at all cost. The administration ultimately chose to end the bilateral dialogue with Iran, and

2

ignored its offer of a grand bargain proposal to settle differences and resume diplomatic relations. This policy decision was at best based on the same errors of mutual misunderstanding and policy miscalculation that have plagued the relationship between the United States and Iran since 1953, and was at worst a victim of policy neglect and hubris after tactical military victory in Afghanistan and Iraq.

CONTEXT

Iran is seven thousand years old. From the height of Persian glory under Darius, Iran survived Greek conquest, defied the Roman Empire, and absorbed the rise of Islam. This legacy weighs heavily on the self-consciousness of most Iranians. Kenneth Pollack, in his masterful analysis of U.S.-Iran relations entitled *The Persian Puzzle*, labels this phenomenon the "persistence of memory," and suggests that in order to understand the complicated nature of relations between both countries, one must first understand the Persian world view.[1] Iran descends from a long tradition of great rulers and magnificent empires. The kingdom of Darius the Great in the sixth-century B.C. was the world's first great superpower, known for its tradition of monotheism, military might, cultural splendor, and bureaucratic innovation. Since the rise of Islam in the sixth-century A.D., Iran has also been the only true Shia Muslim state with a majority Shia population and Shia state religion. Finally, one must recognize that for the past 150 years, Iran has been dominated by powerful regional and extra-regional hegemons, a source of intense national humiliation. According to Pollack, this "reinforced a powerful sense of xenophobia coupled with an inferiority complex among Iranians to complement their superiority complex."[2]

---

[1]Kenneth Pollack, *The Persian Puzzle: The Conflict Between Iran and America* (New York: Random House, 2004), xix, 3.

[2]Ibid., 3-4.

Iran and the Great Game

Persia, as it was then known, was first introduced to the great game of European realpolitik during the late eighteenth-century. In 1796, when the Qajar tribe consolidated power and claimed control of the Persian throne, European nations were encroaching on what had been traditional Persian hegemony. Soon after, the Qajari shah allowed the British East India Company commercial rights at the Persian Gulf port city of Bushehr. In 1804, in what began as a dispute over traditional Persian hegemony in the strategic Caucasus region (Armenia, Azerbaijan, Georgia, and ports on the Caspian and Black Seas), Russia and Persia fought several wars for control of the region. After several military defeats, the Qajari shah was desperate for a European alliance, and soon signed treaties with France and Great Britain (neither of which were fully honored). But Persia soon fell prey to internal European politics, as Russia, France and Britain continuously fought for control of the continent. In 1814, a humiliated shah was forced to sign the Golestan Treaty, the first of many humiliating concessions to European powers.[3]

Throughout the remainder of the nineteenth-century, military defeat, government inefficiency, and political corruption increased Persian dependence on Europe. The shah granted obscene economic concessions to pay off debt and fund his extravagant lifestyle, policies that alienated two influential groups within Iranian society: the *ulema* (Islamic scholars and clerics) and *bazaaris* (traditional merchants and businessmen). Both groups in turn demanded better political representation to counter government inefficiency and corruption. Thus Persia was introduced as a pawn into the great game of European power politics that would last for the next two centuries. These experiences shaped the Persian narrative of the West: international

---

[3] Ali M. Ansari, *Confronting Iran: The Failure of American Foreign Policy and the Next Great Crisis in the Middle East* (New York: Basic Books, 2006), 9-11; Elton Daniel, *The History of Iran* (Westport, CT: Greenwood Press, 2001) 102-104; Pollack, 13-14.

diplomacy was subject to the wider interests of a duplicitous politico-economic system, of which

Iran was not a player but a resource to be exploited.[4]

Constitutional Democracy

From 1905-1906, Persia's educated and *bazaari* classes, with the support of the *ulema*,

demanded political reform. Widespread demonstrations in support of a constitutional movement

forced the shah to create a national parliament, the Majles, which immediately drafted and

approved a national constitution. Persia's fledgling constitutional movement (particularly

economic reforms proposed by the new Majles), however, threatened traditional Russian and

British interests in the region, primarily oil. In 1908, when the Anglo-Persian Oil Company

(APOC) struck oil, Russia and Great Britain sent military forces to occupy their traditional zones

of influence, which led to civil war between Persia's constitutionalists and monarchists. In 1911,

the European powers intervened; with the prospect of war on the horizon, European access to

Persian oil was more important than Persian sovereignty. The Majles was dissolved and the

shah's young grandson assumed the throne. World War I eventually exploited Persian resources

to the breaking point and destroyed its fledgling economy. In the aftermath, the shah sent

emissaries to the Versailles Conference to seek compensation and demonstrate Persian

sovereignty, but they were ignored. After more than a century of exploitation, Persians now

viewed Western interests with suspicion and as the primary source of national humiliation for

their once great nation.[5]

---

[4]Ansari, 12-13; Daniel, 118-121; Nickie R. Keddie, *Modern Iran: Roots and Results of Revolution* (New Haven, CT: Yale University Press, 2003), 36, 43.

[5]Ansari, 15-16, 20-21; Daniel, 121-122; Pollack, 22-26.

World War II and the Cold War: A New Shah

In 1921, Iran was again on the verge of civil war when Reza Khan, commander of Persia's famed Cossack Brigade, seized control of Tehran and quickly consolidated power. Crowned Reza Shah in 1926, he embarked on an ambitious program of modernization and reform to rebuild the nation and revitalize Persian hegemony. In 1935, he changed the name of Persia to Iran, but this was a superficial construct; by the late 1930's, Reza Shah's new Iran was still a hostage of competing European interests. Just as before, World War II was a humiliating experience for Iran. In 1941, fearing a potential Iran-Germany alliance, the Allied Powers occupied Iran to protect their strategic source of oil and overland access to the Soviet Union. Disgraced, Reza Shah abdicated the throne in September, and in his place the Allies installed his weaker son, Mohammad Reza Pahlavi. As a result, Iran's prime minister and the reinstituted Majles gained significant political power. The war devastated Iran's countryside, destroyed the economy, and depleted Iranian resources, reversing the very modest improvements made before the war. By 1946, Iran was still one of the poorest nations in the world.[6]

As British influence waned after the war, the United States soon allied itself with the new shah as a bulwark against the threat of the Soviet Union and budding communist influence within Iranian society. Through this new alliance, the United States would contain the external Soviet threat while the shah focused on domestic issues, particularly control over the growing influence of the prime minister and Majles. The shah's corruption and brutality, however, and nationwide opposition to British oil concessions galvanized a new political coalition to form around an ardent Persian nationalist within the Majles: Mohammad Mosaddeq. Mosaddeq's National Front

---

[6]Ansari, 21-24; Daniel, 131-141; Pollack, 28-37, 48-49.

coalition was a powerful new political force composed of middle class nationalists, *bazaari* businessmen, and the *ulema*. [7]

By 1950, the Anglo-Iranian Oil Company (AIOC), formerly the Anglo-Persian Oil Company, had become the primary symbol of foreign exploitation and national humiliation for the Iranian people. When the National Front gained majority control of the Majles in 1951, they voted to nationalize AIOC; when the prime minister rejected this proposal, he was assassinated, and the politically vulnerable shah was forced to appoint Mosaddeq as prime minister. On April 28, 1951, the Majles passed legislation nationalizing Iran's oil industry, a watershed moment in modern Iranian history. The British government immediately protested: they brought the issue to the International Court of Justice, the United Nations Security Council (UNSC), and began planning for a military invasion of southern Iran. The British also boycotted Iranian oil, froze Iranian assets, and established a naval blockade in the Persian Gulf. In his argument before the UNSC, Mosaddeq successfully argued Iran's case before an international audience. Mosaddeq presumed the United States would support Iran's position, but he underestimated American loyalty to the United Kingdom (in 1951, the United States was embroiled in the Korean conflict and could not afford to alienate their strongest ally). The British government convinced many nations, including the United States, to refuse Iranian requests for financial assistance, a decision that only reinforced the view among many Iranians that America was equally at fault for imperialist injustices imposed on Iran for the last two centuries. [8]

America's response only served to strengthen Mosaddeq at the expense of the shah. In 1952, after British efforts to rig Iranian elections failed, Mosaddeq declared martial law. His drastic measures alienated the core of his constituency, the *ulema* and *bazaari* classes, and

---

[7] Ansari, 24; Daniel, 143-150; Pollack, 48-49.

[8] Ansari, 30-33; Daniel, 148-153; Pollack, 55-64.

threatened the unity of his National Front. In turn, Mosaddeq courted members of Iran's

communist *Tudeh* party to generate political support, and in May 1953, in a desperate attempt to

convince the United States to provide financial aid, publicly threatened an alliance with the

Soviet Union if refused by the West. For the newly elected Eisenhower administration, focused

on the Cold War, this threat from an upstart, erratic Iranian politician could not be tolerated. The

United States preferred order in Iran, and didn't care who kept that order, so long as it contained

Soviet ambitions in the region. [9]

The 1953 Coup

Under continuing pressure from the British government, and with a recommendation

from the CIA station in Tehran, President Eisenhower decided to support the shah over

Mosaddeq. During the summer of 1953, British and American agents in Iran fomented

demonstrations and financed journalist propaganda to undermine the Mosaddeq government.

After the CIA gained the shah's approval for the operation (who promptly fled Iran in case of

failure), CIA officers in Tehran directly coordinated the process of removing the still popular

prime minister. On August 19, 1953, Iranian military units surrounded the prime minister's

residence, and after a short but violent battle, arrested Mosaddeq. The shah returned to the throne

three days later; Mosaddeq was charged with treason, and spent the remainder of his life under

house arrest. [10]

The oil nationalization controversy and the overthrow of Mosaddeq were defining

moments for Iran in the twentieth-century. For Americans, the events were part of the larger Cold

War experience and are now irrelevant. For Iranians, these events shaped a common view of the

United States, however incorrect it may be, that the United States was and is the source of all of

[9] Ansari, 27-35; Daniel, 152-153; Pollack, 60-66.
[10] Ansari, 35-36; Daniel, 153-154; Pollack, 65-67.

Iran's problems. According to Ali Ansari, "It is as if all the foreign machinations of the previous one hundred and fifty years are symbolized by this single event."[11] The collective injustices of the previous two centuries culminated in 1953, and to the benefit of the United Kingdom and the Soviet Union, the United States was in the wrong place at the wrong time. In Iran, the anniversary of the oil nationalization act is an Iranian national holiday, akin to an Iranian Fourth of July.[12] The events of 1953 also served to create a revisionist history of Mosaddeq. As Kenneth Pollack explains, "Like John F. Kennedy's among Americans, the myth of Mohammad Mosaddeq, and of the utopia that he would have created had he survived in power, has become a fixture in Iran's political imagination."[13] Regardless of the truth, the fact is most Iranians believe the United States is solely responsible for the events of 1953, and this belief is so deeply engrained in Iranian society that there is no point arguing to the contrary. Yet the most instructive lesson of 1953 was the importance of religion in Iranian society. The ayatollahs were crucial bases of support for Mosaddeq, and only when those clerics voiced their opposition was the prime minister truly politically vulnerable. The value of pairing the Shia brand of Islam with the Iranian national identity was a political lesson the shah never fully grasped and most Americans never noticed.[14]

The Pahlavi Era

Unfortunately, American foreign policy in Iran after 1953 only served to cement many of the above myths. The United States formed a close relationship with the shah, who in return for financial aid and military assistance, served as a bulwark against Soviet influence in the region. In early 1963, the shah introduced a series of economic and social reforms he called *The Revolution*

---

[11] Ansari, 37.

[12] Ibid.

[13] Pollack, 68.

[14] Daniel, 156.

of the Shah and the People, otherwise known as the *White Revolution*. But these reform measures threatened the traditional power structures of Persian society, particularly the *ulema*. Then in March, a relatively unknown cleric, Ruhollah Khomeini, boldly criticized the shah's reforms and led public protests. He was arrested on June 5, 1963, but nationwide protests in support of Khomeini had the opposite effect, significantly increasing his national visibility and credibility. In October 1964, the Majles narrowly approved a straightforward Status of Forces Agreement with the United States that guaranteed American military personnel diplomatic immunity. Two weeks later, when the United States gave Iran a $200 million military assistance loan, Khomeini denounced the arrangement as a capitulation, reminiscent of British oil concessions. Khomeini was the loudest critic of the shah's corruption and American intervention, and emerged overnight as the voice of Iran's conscience. On November 4, 1964, Khomeini was arrested again, only this time sent into exile in Najaf, Iraq for the next 15 years. [15]

As Iran became more self-sufficient, the shah's relationship with the United States changed—the United States suddenly needed Iran more than Iran needed it. A period of sudden economic growth empowered the shah, who finally felt secure enough to emerge from the shadow of the West and assume the role of a regional hegemon in the Persian Gulf. Reinforcing this strategy, President Nixon applied his Nixon Doctrine to the Middle East, a policy shift that relied on the use of allied proxies to ensure regional security while the United States focused directly on the Soviet Union. In the Middle East, this was known as the *Twin Pillars* policy, whereby the United States would rely on Saudi Arabia and Iran to promote regional stability and protect American interests. The shah also flexed his newfound muscle through the Organization of the Petroleum Exporting Countries: he manipulated world oil markets to increase the global price of oil, and finance what he termed Iran's *Great Civilization*. The price of oil climbed from

---

[15]Ansari, 46-49, 52-53; Daniel, 156-158; Pollack, 76-77, 86, 93-94.

approximately two dollars a barrel in 1971 to approximately $12 a barrel in 1973, and by 1975 Iranian oil revenue rose to $20 billion. Increased revenue opened new possibilities: the shah could now afford to buy the military of his father's dreams, and the United States was more than willing to sell it to him under the Nixon Doctrine. Between 1972 and 1976, the United States sold Iran $10.4 billion worth of weaponry, and by 1976, Iran had one of the largest military forces in the world.[16]

Seeds of Discontent

For all the benefits of this vast new oil wealth, most Iranians only saw a façade. The effects of the shah's White Revolution were disastrous: poor urban planning, combined with population growth, led to a housing shortage which contributed to significant inflation. To make matters worse, foreign corporations fulfilling the regime's contracts brought in over 300,000 foreign workers to fill job requirements. This only increased feelings of xenophobia and served to reinforce the popular perception of Western exploitation of Iranian society. The corrupt government bureaucracy, now flush with capital, became even more corrupt. For Iran's middle class, the shah's policies were disastrous: rising inflation reduced salaries, erased savings, and increased the gap between wealthy Pahlavi loyalists and the urban masses.[17]

In turn, a new Iranian socio-political concept began to flourish: influenced by common discontent among political dissidents and the *ulema*, many argued that Shia Islam and traditional Iranian cultural values were the solution to Iran's continued problems caused by Western influence. An increasingly educated and politically astute younger generation, along with Iran's embattled professional middle class, began to subscribe to this ideology. Iranian peasants, fresh

---

[16]Ansari, 56-66; James A. Bill, *The Eagle and the Lion: The Tragedy of American-Iranian Relations* (New Haven, CT: Yale University Press, 1988), 200-203; Daniel, 159-161.

[17]Bill, 216-217; Pollack, 110-117.

from the countryside, flocked to the mosques and embraced this message from the *ulema*. As Kenneth Pollack summarizes, "In Iran, the economic and physical dislocation that many Iranians experienced, coupled with their sudden exposure to the strange and uncomfortable world of the West, caused many to seek refuge in something traditional and comfortable: Islam."[18] Differing opposition movements flourished underground, composed of former National Front members, the former communist *Tudeh* party, disillusioned college students, professionals, and intellectuals. Between 1965 and 1970, guerilla resistance movements grew, carrying out violent attacks targeting the Pahlavi regime: the Marxist *Mujahedin-e Khalq* (MeK) and Islamist *Fedaiyan-e Khalq*. These two groups, and their ideological divide, represented the future of Iran. Former National Front activists soon formed political organizations that also split along ideological lines: secular and Islamist. The Islamist wing, led by members of the growing Liberation Movement (notably Mehdi Bazargan), was unique in its support for and from the *ulema*. This new political philosophy merged the growing narratives (or myths) of both Mosaddeq's and Khomeini's victimization by interfering Western powers and their puppet government in Tehran. The new Liberation Movement was committed to three principles: (1) that Shia Islam was the solution to Iran's social, political, and economic problems; (2) Shia Islam was compatible with modern society and as such should participate in a representative government; (3) the Pahlavi regime must be overthrown, and nothing short of a revolution was acceptable.[19]

Revolution

By the late 1970s, Iran was effectively a police state controlled by the shah's secret police, SAVAK. When dissidents or clerics spoke out, they were arrested, imprisoned, tortured, and even executed. From Iraq, the Ayatollah Khomeini espoused a progressive form of Shia

---

[18]Pollack, 118.

[19]Bill, 218; Daniel, 161-164.

Islam that made him popular with the younger, disillusioned generation of Iranians, and allowed

him to merge two powerful forces within Iranian society, the middle class and the *ulema*, against

the regime. Khomeini further galvanized public opinion by arguing that since the United States

empowered the shah, America was the source of all evil in Iran. This philosophy was matched by

the extreme xenophobia many Iranians felt towards the many foreign workers employed by

foreign corporations in Iran.[20]

When President Carter visited Iran at the end of 1977 and toasted the shah's "enlightened

leadership," Khomeini decried American hypocrisy regarding the shah's deplorable human rights

record. Ensuing demonstrations in the Iranian religious center of Qom, where government

security forces killed several clerics while dispersing the crowds, set off a chain reaction that

continued for the next year. Public observances mourning the dead turned into protests, resulting

in more deaths, followed by more observances, more violence, and more deaths. In September

1978, Khomeini changed tactics and called for the Iranian people to strike in order to immobilize

Iran's economy and government. Then in October, Khomeini moved to Paris, where international

media coverage only increased his visibility within Iran. This sparked even more protests, and

during the Shia holy days in December 1978, millions of Iranians protested against the regime.

The embattled shah, despite declaring martial law and forming a new government, recognized his

fate, and on January 16, 1979, he left Iran, never to return. Two weeks later, on February 1, 1979,

the Ayatollah Khomeini landed in Tehran, greeted by millions of anxious Iranians. Two weeks

later he appointed Mehdi Bazargan as Iran's new prime minister, and two months later declared

Iran the first Islamic Republic.[21]

---

[20]Ansari, 77; Pollack, 119.
[21]Bill, 234-243, 263; Daniel, 161-164, 183.

Amongst the various factions competing for power in post-revolutionary Iran, Khomeini quickly became the final arbiter for any decision. To further consolidate his influence, Khomeini recognized that the unifying theme among many revolutionaries was a hatred of Western influence, and as such, redefined the goal of the revolution from merely just the removal of the shah to a complete removal of American influence in internal Iranian affairs. Moderation in this respect was viewed as a betrayal of the revolution, and allowed Khomeini to further consolidate his influence over the direction of the revolution and the new Iranian state. Khomeini's political philosophy was based on the concept of *velayat-e faqih*, translated as "rule of the jurisprudent." In this concept of governing, Iran would fall under the rule of a wise member of the *ulema*, a *Faqih* (or Supreme Leader), based on a system of law enshrined in Shia Islam.[22]

From February 1979 until June 1981, Khomeini, as *Faqih*, appointed relatively liberal, moderate politicians who favored continued relations with the United States, albeit a completely different relationship than existed prior to the revolution. Mehdi Bazargan and Abol Hassan Bani-Sadr, both revolutionaries and moderates, served respectively as the first prime minister and president of post-revolutionary Iran. Yet the appointment of both moderates to lead the transitional government masked an on-going battle below the surface of Iranian politics. Within the new Revolutionary Council (composed of seven clerics, seven politicians, and two military officers) and the new Islamic Republic Party (the unifying political body of the radical clerics), the moderates were slowly losing ground to Islamic hardliners; subsequent U.S. policy decisions only accelerated this process.[23]

---

[22]Pollack, 144-146.
[23]Bill, 263-267; Daniel, 184-189.

America: Lost in the Revolution

Amidst the violence and confusion that followed the shah's departure, American

diplomats in Tehran did not know who the major opposition players were. For the previous

decade, American assessments of internal Iranian politics were informed exclusively by the

shah's advisors, who intentionally misled the Americans. As political scientist James Bill

observed,

> The situation in Iran after the revolution, therefore, was extremely sensitive and required
> a delicate and creative diplomatic approach. Given the history of America's political
> involvement in Iran, it was essential that the United States not take any actions that would
> feed this Iranian paranoia, which had considerable basis in fact.[24]

One narrative popular in Washington during this time portrayed the events as a Soviet inspired

communist revolution, and even characterized Khomeini as a communist sympathizer.

Unfortunately, at the White House and in the State Department, those who had long supported the

shah were still shaping U.S. foreign policy in Iran. Further reinforcing this position, many Pahlavi

loyalists, now in the United States, painted themselves as civilized Persians and the

revolutionaries as fanatical Iranians.[25]

Even before the shah left Iran, the Carter administration was considering options for post-

revolutionary Iran. President Carter initially decided the best short-term option required the

Iranian military to assume control, and on January 4, 1979, General Robert Huyser arrived in

Tehran to coordinate efforts with the Iranian military. It was not long, however, before Huyser

realized this was not an option; too many soldiers were deserting, and many officers supported

the revolutionary cause. Ironically, just as many Iranians suspected, the United States was

attempting to undermine the revolution. President Carter's initial policy decisions regarding post-

revolutionary Iran, largely driven by Khomeini's anti-American rhetoric, ultimately reinforced a

---

[24]Bill, 277.

[25]Ansari, 82; Bill, 276-277.

narrative of American interference and intent to control Iran, and shaped U.S.-Iran relations for the next decade.[26]

Faced with no other options, the Carter administration decided to cautiously engage the moderate leaders of Iran's revolutionary government. This approach, however, was not comprehensive. The Carter administration refused to express support for or approval of the revolution, intentionally ignored the Islamist clerics, and tried to isolate Khomeini. In this respect, American policy was flawed, and only served to reinforce Khomeini's suspicions of the United States. In the words of one State Department Iran desk officer,

> How could we hope to establish relations with a country by ignoring its leader? It was illusory to attempt to work with the government while at the same time refusing to have anything to do with the Imam. The government had no power. Khomeini had the power.[27]

Many in the Tehran embassy, however, continued to argue for the administration to expand its policy and engage the clerics.[28]

In May 1979, the U.S. Charge d'Affaires in Tehran, Charles Naas, finally received approval to meet with Khomeini (arranged through Prime Minister Bazargan), but this meeting was cancelled at the last minute due to a May 17, 1979 Senate Resolution condemning the execution of Pahlavi loyalists. The Javits Resolution (as it has since come to be known) was the first of many unfortunate messaging errors that shaped U.S.-Iran relations throughout 1979 and 1980. The resolution triggered more anti-American protests in Iran, and Iran responded by refusing to admit the new American ambassador. In August 1979, the new U.S. Charge d'Affaires in Tehran argued for a policy shift, and the embassy requested an official statement in support of the new government. In September, an internal State Department policy recommendation to Secretary of State Cyrus Vance proposed the administration send a message through Iranian

---

[26]Pollack, 146-148.

[27]Bill, 281.

[28]Ibid., 276-285.

channels requesting another meeting with Khomeini. Ultimately none of these requests were approved because the administration failed to appreciate Khomeini's influence within the revolutionary government. In another messaging mishap, Senator Henry Jackson, during an October 1979 interview on *Meet the Press*, predicted the Iranian revolution would fail, and many Iranians simply assumed his statement was official U.S. policy.[29]

444 Days

On October 22, 1979, President Carter admitted the shah into the United States for cancer treatment, but miscalculated the Iranian reaction. To most Iranians, this signaled continued American support for the shah, who they still feared might return as part of an American supported coup. Spontaneous protests erupted across Iran demonizing the United States. Then on November 1st, Iranian Prime Minister Mehdi Bazargan met with National Security Advisor Zbigniew Brzezinski in Algiers to discuss the future of U.S.-Iran military contracts. Bazargan, although closely allied with the Islamists, was a liberal technocrat, and the type of politician the State Department hoped would govern the new Iranian state. To Iran's paranoid revolutionaries, however, it appeared as if America was conspiring against the new government.[30]

On November 4, 1979, several hundred students from the University of Tehran overran the U.S. Embassy in Tehran, seized 66 American hostages, and demanded the United States return the shah to Iran to be tried for crimes against the Iranian people. After Khomeini publicly endorsed the students, the incident marginalized Bazargan (due to the publicity of his meeting with Brzezinski), who could not intervene or risk appearing as an instrument of U.S. policy; he tendered his resignation to Khomeini on November 6th. This event effectively ended any possibility for the United States to develop a relationship with Khomeini. Ironically, the seizure

---

[29]Ansari, 85-86; Bill, 281-285.
[30]Ansari, 87; Daniel, 190-191.

of the embassy and subsequent hostage crisis was never a goal of the new government. Few recall

that in February 1979, when students first overran the embassy, it was Khomeini and other

Islamist clergy who denounced the attack, and organized students from Tehran University to free

the hostages and restore American control of the facility. It was subsequent U.S. policy decisions

and convoluted messaging that convinced Iranians, particularly Khomeini, that the United States

could not be trusted.[31]

The hostage crisis galvanized public opinion in the United States, and for most

Americans, the embassy crisis was a first impression of Iran. For Iranians, it represented the

success of the revolution, solidified Khomeini's support base, and served as revenge for the 1953

coup. On November 12, 1979, Khomeini demanded four American concessions before the

hostages would be released: Iran wanted all the shah's international assets, his return to face trial,

an American apology for crimes against Iran, and a pledge to refrain from interference in Iranian

affairs. In response, the Carter administration stopped the import of Iranian oil, froze $12 billion

of Iranian assets in U.S. banks, and in April 1980 enacted a trade embargo with Iran. Further

action by the International Criminal Court that same month ordered Iran to free the hostages, but

to no avail. Running out of options, the Carter administration was desperate to find a solution. On

April 24, 1980, U.S. special operations forces attempted a daring raid to rescue the American

hostages. The rescue attempt ended in disaster when eight Americans died in a helicopter

accident in the Iranian desert while attempting to refuel for the flight to Tehran. As a result, the

administration was forced to pursue strictly diplomatic solutions to end the crisis.[32]

By mid-1980, the hostage crisis had indirectly served its purpose in Iran's revolution. The

crisis empowered the Islamists over the moderates, galvanized popular opinion behind Khomeini,

---

[31]Bill, 295-296; Daniel, 190-191; Pollack, 153

[32]Pollack, 164, 169; Robin B. Wright, ed. *The Iran Primer: Power, Politics, and U.S. Policy* (Washington, DC: United States Institute of Peace, 2010), 115, 129-132.

crystallized the myth of American intent to thwart the goals of the revolution, and served as retribution. After the Iranians signaled their intent to release the hostages, negotiations were brokered by the Algerian government, and resulted in the Algiers Accords, signed on January 19, 1981. Under the terms of the agreement, both sides agreed to significant concessions once the hostages were released. Most important for Iran, however, was the agreement that the United States would no longer intervene in Iran's internal affairs.[33]

Downfall of the Moderates

One must remember in evaluating Iran's behavior during this period, that the average Iranian consistently demonstrated a fantastic, gross overestimation of American power and influence, not only in Iran but the greater Middle East. According to former hostage Charles Scott, "It was a situation where truth didn't matter. Perceptions were much more important. A large portion of the Iranian people believed that the United States had the ability to pull strings and return the Shah to power."[34] After the embassy takeover, the students recovered CIA and State Department cables that confirmed their suspicions of covert U.S. interference, weakened the moderate's influence in the transitional government, and destroyed what remained of America's reputation in Tehran. Two incidents in particular contributed to this obsessive paranoia.[35]

In 1978, the U.S. ambassador to Iran, William Sullivan, directed his staff to contact members of the Iranian opposition movement in order to gain a better understanding of what was actually happening in Iran. The embassy contacted representatives of the Liberation Movement, and American diplomats met with Mehdi Barzagan three times in 1978. After the revolution this

---

[33]Bill, 303; Pars Times, "Algiers Accords, January 19, 1981," www.parstimes.com/history/algiers_accords.pdf (accessed March 1, 2013); Wright, *The Iran Primer: Power, Politics, and U.S. Policy*, 115.

[34]Tim Well, *444 Days: The Hostages Remember* (San Diego: Harcourt Brace Jovanovich, 1985), 28-29.

[35]Bill, 285-293.

channel became critical, since most of these contacts were in positions of leadership within the new government. The relationship became so strong that between August and October 1979, CIA officers provided intelligence briefings to key members of the transitional government, including Prime Minister Bazargan, the foreign minister, and the deputy prime minister.[36]

In early 1979, a CIA officer under commercial cover approached Abol Hassan Bani-Sadr in Paris. Bani-Sadr, like Bazargan, was a moderate liberal, but he was also Khomeini's closest advisor during the final days of the revolution. The case officer was Vernon Cassin, who claimed to be an international businessman interested in Iranian business opportunities. Over the course of several meetings, Bani-Sadr agreed to meet with Cassin later that year in Tehran. When Bani-Sadr returned to Iran with Khomeini in February 1979, he was appointed to the influential Revolutionary Council and Assembly of Experts (responsible for drafting a new constitution). In August 1979, Cassin traveled to Tehran and offered Bani-Sadr a consulting fee for providing Cassin's "corporate backers" with assessment information on Iranian political developments.[37]

In both operations, CIA officers documented the meetings and assigned code names for each Iranian contact. Both incidents, and the secret documentation recovered at the embassy, not only destroyed the influence of the moderates in the Islamic Republic, but also ruined any potential for a diplomatic solution to the hostage crisis. For Bazargan, recently resigned as prime minister, he quickly lost what credibility he had left within revolutionary circles, and Bani-Sadr's critics used these documents to continually discredit him. According to James Bill,

> It also reinforced the views of Iranian revolutionaries that the United States had every intention of taking control of the revolution itself. In their eyes, this was clear and incontrovertible evidence that the shah's admission into the United States was part of an overall plot to weaken and ultimately overturn the Iranian revolution.[38]

---

[36]Ibid., 290-291.

[37]Ibid., 286-287.

[38]Ibid., 288, 297.

The Algiers Accords effectively ended U.S.-Iran relations for the next several years and set the tone of the relationship for the next three decades. In the immediate aftermath of the revolution, U.S. foreign policy in Iran failed for several reasons. First, the Carter administration waited too long after the shah's departure to develop a relevant Iran policy. Once the administration developed a policy of cautious engagement, American diplomats and intelligence officers were unable to provide an accurate picture of post-revolutionary Iran, and the administration failed to publicly acknowledge the revolution or establish contact with Khomeini. Further complicating matters, the administration clumsily orchestrated efforts to establish relationships with moderate Iranian leaders, such as Brzezinski's ill-advised Algiers meeting with Prime Minister Bazargan, and the CIA's brazen efforts to recruit Bani-Sadr and other moderates in the transitional government. These efforts only served to undermine the influence of the moderates within the revolutionary government, and strengthen the control of Islamic hardliners in the new regime.

Just as the 1953 coup established the basis for U.S.-Iran relations from Iran's perspective, the 1979 revolution and ensuing hostage crisis framed U.S.-Iran relations for the United States. As Ali Ansari describes, "For adherents to Iran's revolutionary ideology, the Islamic Revolution indicates a definitive break with the past, defined by the termination of relations with the United States."[39] For Iranians, the seizure of the U.S. Embassy was the coup de main of their enduring struggle against 200 years of foreign intervention and exploitation. After the crisis ended, although most Iranians considered the matter settled and were prepared to move on, the American public did not agree. Iran had humiliated the United States. For most Americans, the televised images of the hostages and burning American flags, combined with vehement anti-American

---

[39] Ansari, 71.

21

political and spiritual ideology, marked the beginning of a new era in U.S.-Iran relations, one of Iranian revolutionary hostility towards an innocent America.

EARLY EFFORTS AT RAPPROCHEMENT

While Presidents Reagan, Bush, and Clinton were forced to deal with the Iran dilemma, each administration also tried to improve relations through varied policy approaches. These attempts failed for numerous reasons, but foremost because the United States and Iran lacked formal diplomatic relations. The severance of diplomatic relations only bred foreign policies based on mutual distrust, ignorance, and paranoia. Another consequence was the loss of Iranian expertise within the State Department. For the next two decades, Iran policy decisions were often based on incomplete or inaccurate information. Iran policy was also rarely a priority, but instead an issue to be managed or contained. Further complicating matters, the Algiers Accords of 1981 were never ratified in the United States, which led some to challenge the legal status of the clause regarding non-interference in Iran's internal affairs. This legal nuance only encouraged American intervention and convinced Iran's hardliner revolutionaries that the United States would continue to do everything in its power to undermine the revolution. With no diplomatic relations to avert miscommunication, and in the absence of a clearly articulated Iran policy, U.S. policy decisions from 1980 to 2000 ultimately isolated and antagonized the Islamic Republic.[40]

When the new administration took office in January 1981, President Reagan was primarily focused on domestic policy and the Soviet Union. But with the shah gone, America was vulnerable in the Middle East, and no one in the administration wanted to push Iran towards the Soviets. Wisely, the administration initially adopted a hands-off policy of indifference, but that

---

[40]Ibid., 99, 102-103; Evan Usher, "A Series of Missed Opportunities—The Algiers Accords," *American Iranian Council News*, August 31, 2012, http://american-iranian.org/print/644 (accessed January 17, 2013).

would not last long. Two events initially shaped U.S.-Iran relations throughout the Reagan administration: the Iran-Iraq war and Israel's invasion of Lebanon in 1982.[41]

The Iran-Iraq War

Immediately after the revolution, Khomeini created the Islamic Revolutionary Guards Corps (IRGC), or *Pasdaran* units, to serve as a paramilitary force responsible for maintaining order and defending the principles of the revolution. The IRGC became a political weapon for the clerics, who used it to purge the government and military of moderates and dissidents, but the IRGC's influence would soon spread beyond Iran's borders. The preamble of Iran's new constitution called for the spread of the Islamic Revolution around the Muslim world, and Khomeini exhorted Muslims elsewhere to rise up against their own "shahs," in particular Saddam Hussein. To facilitate the spread of the revolution, Iran formed an Office of Liberation Movements (OLM), which oversaw financial and military support for foreign Shia dissident groups.[42]

When Iraq invaded Iran in September 1980, many Iranians were convinced the attack was an international assault on the revolution, an imposed war of good versus evil. To rally the population, Khomeini used the symbolism of the 1979 Soviet invasion of Afghanistan and the 1980 Baathist invasion of Iran to frame the conflict as a struggle between the satanic superpowers and the rightful rule of Islam; later U.S. foreign policy decisions would only validate his claim. In 1982, the Iranian army battled back from defeat. Inspired by Iran's mullahs, untrained militias (spin-offs from IRGC *Pasdaran* units), such as the *Hizballahis* and *Basij* corps, walked through mine fields in human wave assaults and overwhelmed the Iraqi army. Despite signals that Iraq was willing to accept a ceasefire and withdraw from Iranian territory, in July 1982 Iranian forces

---

[41]Wright, *The Iran Primer: Power, Politics, and U.S. Policy,* 133-135.

[42]Daniel, 203; Pollack, 151, 183, 198.

launched a massive counterattack. The Iraqi army, however, quickly repulsed this new offensive with a supply of advanced weapons from France and American intelligence revealing Iranian troop movements (provided by the Saudis).[43]

Although the United States officially remained neutral throughout the war, Iran's 1982 offensive alarmed many in the administration, particularly Secretary of State George Schultz and Secretary of Defense Caspar Weinberger. After Khomeini rallied his army with calls to liberate Karbala, Baghdad, and Jerusalem, Reagan decided to intervene. The United States provided Iraq with loans and intelligence, and after Donald Rumsfeld's now infamous visit to Baghdad in 1983, restored diplomatic relations with Iraq on November 26, 1984. President Reagan's support of Iraq, despite proclamations of neutrality, convinced Khomeini the United States was blatantly violating the 1981 Algiers Accords, and still intent on undermining the Islamic Republic. [44]

1982: Israel Invades Lebanon

When Israel invaded Lebanon in June 1982 to expel Yasser Arafat's Palestine Liberation Organization (PLO) from southern Lebanon, Iran's OLM dispatched IRGC militants to Lebanon's Bekaa Valley outside Beirut, to assist the Shia Battalions of Lebanese Resistance (AMAL). The occupation of Lebanon brought the Israeli Defense Forces (IDF) into direct confrontation with a Shia majority that until then peacefully coexisted with Israel. The IDF's heavy-handed tactics, however, soon alienated the local populace and created the perfect opportunity for the IRGC, who offered funding and training for the more extreme factions of AMAL. These groups formed a new movement, Hizbollah, as an operational headquarters for the Islamic revolutionary movement in Lebanon. On August 25, 1982, President Reagan deployed the U.S. Marines as part of a multinational-force (MNF), including British, French and Italian

---

[43]Ansari, 105-107; Bill, 304-307; Daniel, 202-209; Pollack, 183, 196-197, 207-208.
[44]Ansari, 105-107; Bill, 306-307.

peacekeepers, to facilitate the PLO's withdrawal from Beirut and restore order under the new

Christian Lebanese government. American policy in Lebanon supported the legitimate

government, but the Reagan administration never fully appreciated the dynamics of Lebanese

politics, and failed to recognize that most Lebanese factions (e.g., Maronite, Druze, AMAL)

opposed the Christian government. In short, there was no legitimate Lebanese government. For

the Lebanese Shia majority, America's shortsighted policy signaled that the United States had

taken sides, and the Marines became a legitimate target. On April 18, 1983, a truck bomb

detonated outside the U.S. Embassy in Beirut, killing 63, including 17 Americans. Then on

October 23, 1983, truck bombs detonated at the U.S. Marine barracks and the French compound,

killing 241 Marines and 57 French paratroopers. When the United States finally left Lebanon in

early 1984, American prestige in the region was at an all time low.[45]

The 1983 attacks in Lebanon marked the first foreign policy crisis of the Reagan

administration. As the administration debated a proper policy response, a group calling itself

Islamic Jihad claimed credit for the attacks. Secretary Shultz and many within the National

Security Council (NSC) favored a strong military response, but others, notably Secretary

Weinberger, believed U.S. policy in Iran was flawed from the start and opposed it. Ultimately,

President Reagan called off a military response for lack of credible evidence, but that did not stop

many in the administration from accusing Iran. This was compounded again by a lack of reliable

diplomatic and intelligence reporting on Iran and the Islamic revolutionary movement. For many,

this was a logical leap: Druze and Shiite militias attacked the embassy and Marine barracks,

Hizbollah is the new Lebanese Shiite militia, Iran supports Hizbollah, therefore Iran was

responsible. Although there was credible reporting that Lebanese Hizbollah worked with Iranian

officials to plan the attacks, this was never proved. In a September 2001 *Frontline* interview,

---

[45]Pollack, 198-205.

former Secretary of Defense Weinberger admitted the government still lacks any knowledge of who was behind the attacks; Hizbollah still denies responsibility. [46]

American policy in Lebanon was flawed: it had the dubious political objective of maintaining the peace, and was based primarily on America's support of Israel within the UNSC. The Lebanon fiasco further alienated the United States and Iran, and introduced Hizbollah as the new international symbol of fanatical Iranian Islamic terrorism. According to Ali Ansari,

> It also highlighted an emerging trend in American foreign policy judgments: where ambiguity existed, the balance of consensus concluded that Iran must be in some way responsible. The development of such a conspiratorial mentality among American analysts paradoxically ensured that the absence of evidence effectively convicted Iran and ascribed guilt, in a manner that overturned traditional western notions of jurisprudence. [47]

Weapons for Hostages

By 1984, the effects of the war with Iraq brought about an interesting dynamic frequently observed in Iran's internal politics. Despite Khomeini's pursuit of Iran's revolutionary ideal (draconian social policies, export of the revolution, and opposition to the international order), the reality of these policy repercussions occasionally allowed political pragmatists an opportunity to reign in the Islamic hardliners, and make necessary reforms to ensure regime survival. While these radical swings in Iranian political behavior make international relations with Iran difficult and unpredictable, it has provided limited opportunities for rapprochement. The first instance of this dynamic occurred in 1985, when Iran and the United States participated in a bizarre deal to exchange arms for hostages.

By the mid-1980s, the Iranian military, built with American manufactured weapons, was suffering from the U.S. arms embargo. In 1983, the Department of State initiated Operation

---

[46]Ibid.; PBS Frontline, "Target America," http://www.pbs.org/wgbh/pages/frontline/ shows/target/etc/cron.html (accessed March 10, 2013).

[47]Ansari, 102-103.

Staunch, a semi-successful effort to halt the illicit flow of U.S. weaponry via third party sales and the black market. Internally, a struggle ensued between Iran's conservative hardline clerics and pragmatic politicians; the latter argued the best option for regime survival was to end the war with Iraq and reengage the international community, including the United States. By 1984, Majles chairman Ali Akbar Hashemi Rafsanjani, a close confidante of Khomeini, was convinced Iran had to engage the United States for military support.[48]

Between 1982 and 1985, seven American citizens were kidnapped in Lebanon. Although different groups were responsible, they all had ties to Islamic Jihad or Lebanese Hizbollah, and demanded in return the release of Shia militants held by Kuwait. The Reagan administration, however, refused to negotiate for the release of the hostages. So on June 14, 1985, members of Islamic Jihad, led by Lebanese militant Imad Mughniya, hijacked TWA flight 847, executed a U.S. Navy passenger, and demanded the release of several hundred Lebanese Shia prisoners held by Israel. As the crisis escalated, Rafsanjani, with Khomeini's approval, was instrumental in the release of the TWA flight 847 hostages in exchange for Lebanese Shia prisoners later released by Israel. Nevertheless, President Reagan still faced the same dilemma as Carter: what to do about the remaining hostages? Key administration officials, notably National Security Advisor Robert McFarlane and CIA Director William Casey, urged President Reagan to engage Iran, while Secretary of Defense Weinberger and Secretary of State Shultz opposed any policy of engagement. Based on new intelligence indicating Iran was on the brink of collapse and might

[48]Ansari, 109-110; Keddie, 258; Pollack, 211; Kenneth R. Timmerman, "Fanning the Flames: Guns, Greed & Geopolitics in the Gulf War," The Iran Brief, www.iran.org/tib/krt/ fanning_ch7.htm (accessed March 12, 2013).

turn to the Soviets for support, some administration officials hoped that over time, an opportunity

to engage Iran would present itself. Rafsanjani embodied just that opportunity.[49]

Beginning in May 1985, several NSC officials orchestrated a secret policy of limited

rapprochement with Iran in an effort to guarantee the release of the remaining hostages and re-

establish bilateral relations. President Reagan signed a Presidential Finding on January 17, 1986,

authorizing the sale of American weapons to Iran (through Israeli and Iranian intermediaries) for

the release of American hostages. Then, on May 25, 1986, a secret American entourage,

including former National Security Advisor Robert McFarlane and Marine Lt. Col. Oliver North,

landed in Tehran to meet with the Iranians, but the negotiations were fruitless. In a May 26th

report to National Security Advisor John Poindexter, McFarlane complained, "The incompetence

of the Iranian government to do business requires a rethinking on our part of why there have been

so many frustrating failures to deliver on their part."[50] Remarkably, in July 1986, the Iranians

succeeded in opening a second channel of communication with the United States, independent of

Israeli intermediaries, leading directly to Khomeini's office. In direct meetings between

American and Iranian officials in October 1986, the Iranians agreed to work for the release of

some hostages, but made clear that they could not secure the release of all the hostages. This

cooperation, however, quickly evaporated. In October 1986, the story leaked to the press, and

both governments distanced themselves from the entanglement. Ultimately, several Americans

were indicted, while one Iranian, responsible for leaking the story, was arrested and executed.[51]

---

[49]Bill, 311; Keddie, 258; Pollack, 209-210; University of California, Santa Barbara, The American Presidency Project, "Excerpts From the Tower Commission's Report," http://www.presidency.ucsb.edu/PS157/assignment%20files%20public/TOWER%20EXCERPTS .htm (accessed March 15, 2013).

[50]University of California, Santa Barbara.

[51]Ansari, 111; Bill, 308; Keddie, 258; University of California, Santa Barbara.

Unfortunately, this scheme was indicative of the administration's flawed policy approach towards Iran. The United States was still plagued by a lack of Iran policy specialists, and with the State Department opposed to reengagement, they were not included in the decision making process. The decision to engage the Iranians was also based on several faulty assumptions. First, the Israelis convinced administration officials the Iranians could directly influence Hizbollah and guarantee the release of each hostage. Yet despite shipping thousands of missiles and spare parts to Iran, only three hostages were released, but not before more Americans were kidnapped. Next, the administration assumed the intermediaries were credible and spoke for reliable sources within the Iranian government. In fact, the primary intermediary, Manucher Ghobanifar, was a former SAVAK agent and Mossad source whom the CIA considered neither reliable nor trustworthy. Finally, the NSC staff believed the pragmatists in the Iranian government could make substantive change. The administration failed to recognize that Rafsanjani and other pragmatists would face considerable resistance from the regime's hardliners. The worst example of this naivety was an NSC expectation that after the weapons sales, Khomeini would eventually step down as Supreme Leader.[52]

The entire affair, although a foreign policy disaster that nearly ruined Reagan and Rafsanjani, did demonstrate the existence of an emerging realist, pragmatic movement within Iran's political elite. U.S. foreign policy, however, was misguided and poorly coordinated. The administration, in what became known as the *Iran-Contra* affair, clumsily merged diplomatic rapprochement with clandestine operations to sell weapons and recover hostages. As with the CIA's recruitment efforts after the 1979 revolution, the administration failed to consider what would happen to their Iranian counterparts if exposed. "For the U.S. political elite, the lessons included the curious conclusion that Iran had no moderates worth negotiating with, that the

_____

[52]Ansari, 110-111; Bill, 308-309; University of California, Santa Barbara.

system as a whole was rotten, and that the people were duplicitous."[53] Likewise, televised

coverage of Oliver North's congressional testimony claiming he lied every time he met with the

Iranians convinced Iran that American overtures could not be trusted. The events of 1986

ultimately contributed to mutual feelings of distrust and paranoia that set the stage for conflict the

very next year in the Persian Gulf.[54]

The Persian Gulf Tanker War

From 1986 to 1988, the Iran-Iraq War spilled over into the Persian Gulf and finally

brought the United States into direct military confrontation with Iran. The Persian Gulf Tanker

War was a last ditch effort by both sides to cripple the others primary source of revenue: the oil

industry. In July 1987, after Iran attacked several Kuwaiti oil tankers, the U.S. Navy initiated

Operation Earnest Will. American warships escorted (Kuwaiti) re-flagged American oil tankers

through the Persian Gulf, and soon the United States and Iran were engaged in a form of limited

naval warfare: IRGC small boats laid mines in the Gulf, and the U.S. Navy responded with

counter-mine operations. In April 1988, after Iranian mines damaged an American warship, the

U.S. Navy initiated Operation Praying Mantis, directly targeting the Iranian navy. The U.S. Navy

destroyed an Iranian frigate, disabled another, and destroyed several Iranian oil platforms in the

Gulf. Tragically, on July 3, 1988, the U.S.S. *Vincennes* mistakenly shot down a civilian airliner,

Iran Air flight 655, killing all 290 aboard. The Iranians were certain this was an intentional act

that signaled American intent to escalate hostilities if Iran continued the war. With domestic

support for the war waning, Rafsanjani was finally able to convince Khomeini to accept cease-

fire terms on July 20, 1988. Although Khomeini's decision to accept the ceasefire and avoid

---

[53] Ansari, 112.
[54] Bill, 308, 314.

regime collapse demonstrated the growing pragmatic nature of Iranian politics, the effects of the Iran Air incident would continue to haunt U.S.-Iran relations for the next decade.[55]

Reagan: Analysis

The Reagan administration came into office largely ignorant of Iran, but shaped by the events of the 1979 revolution and ensuing hostage crisis, stumbled from indifference to hostility, and from limited cooperation to confrontation. The lack of diplomatic relations after the revolution only reinforced mutual suspicion and distrust. Reagan's decision to support Iraq during its war with Iran further antagonized the Islamic Republic, and the administration's decision to support Israel and intervene in Lebanon led to the emergence of Hizbollah. The arms for hostages effort at rapprochement was predisposed to fail, particularly because rapprochement was not the primary goal for either side, and had the effort been successful, improved relations would have been an unlikely side effect. Reagan's policy decisions were motivated by his humanitarian concern for the hostages, and desire to maintain America's strategic position in the Cold War. For Rafsanjani and Khomeini, this was a dangerous experiment with realism to ensure regime survival. By 1988, the United States was in an undeclared war with Iran, primarily because the administration never developed a coherent Iran policy or a comprehensive strategy to achieve policy ends. The unpredictable nature of Iranian politics, combined with the unique nature of Shia revolutionary ideology, convinced many in the administration that nothing could be done. Ultimately, it would be up to the next administration to develop a realistic Iran foreign policy.

---

[55]Daniel, 216-217; Keddie, 259; Wright, *The Iran Primer: Power, Politics, and U.S. Policy,* 133-135.

<u>From Khomeini to Khamenei</u>

Although Khomeini had managed to consolidate his political power through the support of Iran's conservative clerics, in its first decade Iran's political system had grown decentralized and fragmented. Iran's convoluted political structure made policy consensus difficult, if not impossible, and often empowered individual regime elements to sometimes pursue rogue, freelance foreign policy adventures. The struggle for political power inside Iran revolved primarily around two groups: conservatives and pragmatists. The conservative *ulema*, often described as radicals or hardliners, were the primary base of support for Khomeini. They were the most ardent supporters of the revolution and opposed any rapprochement with the West. Iranian pragmatists differed with the conservatives primarily in the area of foreign policy. The former argued that in order for the republic to survive, it must embrace a more realist foreign policy, reform the economy, and improve relations with the West. By 1988, Rafsanjani and Iranian President Ali Hosseini Khamenei were two of Iran's leading pragmatists who, having convinced Khomeini to end the war with Iraq, were now the most influential politicians in Iran.[56]

In 1988, an ailing Khomeini allowed Khamenei and Rafsanjani to engineer key changes to the Iranian constitution that would empower the next generation of Iranian leadership and ensure regime survival. Khamenei and Rafsanjani, the most likely successors to Khomeini, also moved to improve relations with the West.[57] Through late 1988 and early 1989, in anticipation of improved relations with the new U.S. administration, Iran sent encouraging signals. An Iranian newspaper editorial opined, "We have nothing to lose by establishing proper relations with the superpowers of the West based on justified rights of the Islamic Republic," while an Iranian foreign ministry official acknowledged that if U.S. politicians "change their policies and treat us

---

[56]Daniel, 219-222; Keddie, 260.
[57]Daniel, 222; Pollack, 238.

with mutual respect and nonintervention in our affairs, the relations with the United States will be like that with other countries."[58]

Khomeini died on June 3, 1989, and two days later the Assembly of Experts named President Khamenei as *Faqih*. One month later in a special election, Rafsanjani was overwhelmingly elected to replace Khamenei as president. Thus, Iran's leading pragmatists, instrumental in revising the constitution and reforming the government, now controlled the future of the Islamic Republic. Khamenei was selected not for his religious credentials (he was not yet an ayatollah when appointed *Faqih*), but for his political acumen, so he was forced to maintain a low profile for several years until he consolidated a stronger base of support amongst the more senior clerics. As such, over the next several years, Khamenei emerged much more conservative in order to secure his eventual success as Supreme Leader. Rafsanjani intended to rebuild the nation through economic reforms and improved relations with the West, and stressed a theme that cooperation should replace confrontation in international relations. Rafsanjani's presidency was considered by many as Iran's greatest opportunity yet to realign itself with the international community. [59]

Bush Policy: The Picco Channel

The year 1989 brought about transitions of power within the United States and Iran that many observers hoped would finally usher in an era of improved relations between both nations. U.S. policy towards Iran in 1989 was still shaped primarily by the issue of the remaining hostages in Lebanon, and Iran's support of terrorism abroad through Hizbollah. The Bush administration foreign policy team, led by National Security Advisor Brent Scowcroft, although initially

---

[58]Robin B. Wright, *In the Name of God: The Khomeini Decade* (New York: Simon and Schuster, 1989), 195.

[59]Daniel, 222-226; Keddie, 263-264; Pollack, 241-242.

cautious toward Iran, hoped to improve relations. President Bush initiated this effort through his inaugural address, asking for Rafsanjani's assistance in freeing the remaining hostages and pledging that Iran's assistance would not go unnoticed. He suggested that "good will begets good will," and "good faith can be a spiral that endlessly moves on."[60] Iran in turn, suggested informal talks via Pakistan, but the Bush administration countered with proposed secret meetings in Europe between Iranian and American diplomats. Rafsanjani initially declined; he had barely survived the political aftermath of Iran-Contra, and feared exposure of the meetings would undermine his progressive agenda. President Bush was insistent however, and on August 25, 1989, he sent UN Under-Secretary-General Giandomenico Picco to Tehran to meet with Rafsanjani and deliver a message: in exchange for Iran's assistance in freeing the hostages, the United States would consider normalizing relations and releasing Iranian assets still frozen in U.S. banks. Bush's condition was that because of Iran-Contra, the administration could not do anything until the hostages were released.[61] The Bush administration's new policy of engagement and normalization was documented in National Security Directive 26, signed on October 2, 1989. According to this document,

> The U.S. should continue to be prepared for a normal relationship with Iran on the basis of strict reciprocity. A process for normalization must begin with Iranian action to cease its support for international terrorism and help obtain the release of all American hostages.[62]

Although Rafsanjani informed Picco that Iran lacked direct influence over the Lebanese groups holding the hostages, he did agree to apply pressure, but only if the United States would

---

[60]Bartleby.com, "Inaugural Address of President George H. W. Bush, Friday, January 20, 1989," http://www.bartleby.com/124/pres63.html (accessed March 15, 2013).

[61]Shireen T. Hunter, *Iran's Foreign Policy in the Post-Soviet Era: Resisting the New International Order* (Santa Barbara: Praeger, 2010), 46; Pollack, 246; Wright, *The Iran Primer: Power, Politics, and U.S. Policy*, 137.

[62]Federation of American Scientists—Intelligence Resource Program, "Bush Administration National Security Directive 26: U.S. Policy Toward the Persian Gulf," http://www.fas.org/irp/offdocs/nsd/nsd26.pdf (accessed March 15, 2013).

show good faith first by releasing 10 percent of the seized assets and compensate the families of

Iran Air flight 655. Although the Bush administration never officially responded to Rafsanjani's

counteroffer, Rafsanjani pursued the opportunity in good faith, and in April 1990, two hostages

were released. Yet the issue of rapprochement with Iran still faced stiff opposition in the United

States, particularly with some in the State Department who did not want to reward Iran with

incentives. Ultimately, the Bush administration held back for several reasons. First, Iran was not

able to secure the release of all the hostages. As Rafsanjani admitted to Picco, Iran did not

directly control Lebanese Hizbollah, and some conservative hardliners in the government

continued to use personal connections with the Lebanese groups to manipulate the situation and

undermine Rafsanjani's efforts. Second, rouge regime elements continued to pursue independent

foreign policies. During the early 1990s, several high profile Iranian dissidents living in exile in

Europe were assassinated, reinforcing allegations that Iran still supported international terrorism.

Finally, the opportunity for rapprochement fell victim to world events: the Berlin Wall came

down in 1989, followed by the gradual thaw of relations with and disintegration of the Soviet

Union in 1991. These events monopolized U.S. foreign policy, and Iran was no longer a priority.

When Iraq invaded Kuwait in August 1990, Iran remained neutral and cooperated with the UN

arms embargo, but a decisive U.S. victory through a multinational (including Arab) coalition only

made Iran seem less relevant in the opinion of many U.S. policy makers.[63]

With the Picco channel still open after the Gulf War, the Bush administration tried once

more to improve relations and arrange the release of the remaining hostages. The terms of the

deal were the same, but with one caveat: Rafsanjani must publicly denounce terrorism. In a late

1991 prayer sermon, Rafsanjani condemned terrorism, and the remaining hostages were released

---

[63]Ansari, 126; Shireen T. Hunter, *Iran After Khomeini*, The Washington Papers vol. 156, (New York: Praeger, 1992), 124-125; Hunter, *Iran's Foreign Policy in the Post-Soviet Era: Resisting the New International Order,* 47-49; Pollack, 245-253.

in December. Yet despite Iran fulfilling its end of the bargain, the arrangement ultimately fell victim to American domestic politics and Iran's bipolar foreign policy. In August 1991, Iran's former Prime Minister Shapour Bakhtiar was murdered in Paris, and in September 1992, four Iranian Kurdish dissidents were murdered in Berlin. Investigations implicated rogue elements within Iran's security and intelligence services, and with Bush facing a tough re-election battle against Bill Clinton, he could not afford to risk another Iran scandal or appear to appease Iran. In an April 1992 meeting with Rafsanjani in Tehran, Picco relayed a final message from Scowcroft: President Bush could make no gestures toward Iran because the timing was wrong.[64]

Bush: Analysis

Bush administration efforts at rapprochement failed because of political reasons on both sides. From the American perspective, efforts to normalize relations with Iran were quickly overcome by world events and America's emergence as the lone superpower. After the Gulf War, the United States became a dominant presence forward deployed in the Middle East, and the issue of Iran became a liability for an administration fighting for political survival. Further, the new world order that emerged from the Cold War (and the Gulf War) vindicated the conviction of many U.S. policymakers that Western culture and values were dominant, and should shape the new international system. In the shadow of these developments, Iran was essentially ignored and excluded from regional security plans.

From Iran's perspective, internal disagreements complicated what was already an extremely sensitive issue. Anti-Americanism and the principle of exporting the revolution were the twin pillars of Khomeini's legacy. Although Khamenei and Rafsanjani agreed on domestic issues, over time, Khamenei began to side with the conservatives opposing rapprochement. This

---

[64]Ansari, 126, 131-132; Daniel, 228-234; Hunter, *Iran's Foreign Policy in the Post-Soviet Era: Resisting the New International Order*, 49; Keddie, 266-269.

was less about ideology and more about political survival as *Faqih*. Regardless, the conservatives still had enough influence to constrain the pragmatist's efforts at reconciliation. Further limiting Rafsanjani's effort was the fragmented nature of Iranian politics; he was never able to form a coalition strong enough to break free of the conservative's hold on political power. In the end, the dynamics of Iranian politics ensured that a majority could always agree on what to oppose, restricting any substantive effort to improve relations with the West. As Iranian expert Shireen Hunter observed, "As long as the domestic political debate is not resolved and a solid majority view formed, these problems will bedevil Iran's foreign policy." [65]

Finally, rapprochement was not possible because it fell victim to the lack of diplomatic relations. After both sides rejected multilateral talks and secret negotiations, the dialogue was entrusted to a UN intermediary, and it was no longer a priority, especially for the United States. Further, rapprochement was still not the primary goal of either side. Rafsanjani's attempt to normalize relations with the West was a result of his commitment to improve Iran's economy and rebuild the nation after a decade of war, while American foreign policy regarding Iran was still driven by the hostage crisis in Lebanon. For both governments, rapprochement was never the true end, but merely a potential positive side effect.

Iranian Foreign Policy Transition

Rafsanjani's twice failed effort at rapprochement with the United States cost him politically. Beginning in 1992, powerful individuals in the Iranian government began to engage in freelance diplomacy, facilitating Hizbollah terror attacks and assassinations abroad in a dramatic shift to a much more aggressive foreign policy. Several events caused this shift, not the least of which was Rafsanjani's rebuff by the Bush administration. The post-Gulf War buildup of the U.S. military throughout the Persian Gulf alarmed many Iranian conservatives, who feared a potential

---

[65]Hunter, *Iran After Khomeini*, 136.

U.S. invasion. Between 1991 and 1997, Iran purchased approximately $1.4 billion worth of

military equipment from former Soviet central-Asian governments. In 1995, Iran signed a

contract with Russia to develop a nuclear research reactor at Bushehr, and as the world would

discover years later, restarted its nuclear program under the guidance of Pakistan's notorious Dr.

A.Q. Khan.[66]

Most importantly, the 1991 Madrid Peace Conference (hosted by the United States to

begin an Arab-Israeli peace process) infuriated many hardliners in Iran who refused to recognize

the existence of Israel. Any peace agreement would legitimize Israel, alienate one of Iran's

strongest allies, Syria, and likely force Hizbollah to disarm. Iran opposed the Arab-Israeli peace

process, and in 1992 began encouraging Hizbollah and Palestinian Islamic Jihad to cooperate

with HAMAS, providing millions of dollars in financial support. Between 1992 and 1996,

Hizbollah and its affiliates conducted multiple international terrorist attacks targeting Israeli

diplomatic establishments; most notably several attacks targeting Israelis in Argentina. Iran

expanded its worldwide intelligence networks, notably targeting Israeli and U.S. diplomatic and

military personnel in what many feared might be a prelude to more kidnappings or bombings.

Although Iran was not capable of preventing an Arab-Israeli peace agreement, Iran's rhetoric in

opposing the process, while simultaneously pursuing improved relations with Europe and the

United States, was just another example of its incoherent foreign policy. This bipolar foreign

policy rhetoric only convinced the Israelis that Iran would never accept an Israeli state, and made

it impossible for the United States to consider improved relations with Iran in the short term.[67]

---

[66]GlobalSecurity.org, "Weapons of Mass Destruction: Bushehr Background," http://www.globalsecurity.org/wmd/world/iran/bushehr-intro.htm (accessed March 10, 2013); Hunter, *Iran's Foreign Policy in the Post-Soviet Era: Resisting the New International Order,* 51; Pollack, 253-259.

[67]Hunter, *Foreign Policy in the Post-Soviet Era,* 51; Pollack, 253-256.

Dual Containment

While the new Clinton administration was primarily interested in its domestic agenda as part of a post Cold War peace dividend, the new foreign policy team was extremely focused on the Arab-Israeli peace process. The question of Iran was limited to discussions of how to handle or contain Iran, so as to prevent its influence in regional matters. As discussed previously, the lack of Iranian experts in the U.S. foreign policy and diplomatic establishments still restricted American foreign policy options in the region. As a result, the nuances of Middle East politics were forced to fit theories based on the former Soviet Union, discrepancies were conveniently ignored, and similar policy forecasts made. Many in the Clinton administration were also weary of Iranian efforts at reconciliation. Secretary of State Warren Christopher was shaped primarily by his experiences dealing with the Iranians during the 1980-1981 Algiers Accords negotiations. National Security Advisor Anthony Lake was hesitant to engage the Iranians because of the experiences of the Bush administration and the nature of Iran's bipolar foreign policy. The result was the Clinton administration's policy of *Dual Containment*: the United States basically drew a box around Iran and Iraq, and hoped that with time and pressure, both regimes would inevitably collapse.[68]

In a March 18, 1993, speech before the Washington Institute for Near East Policy, Assistant Secretary of State Martin Indyk introduced the policy of Dual Containment to contain both Iran and Iraq, independently and via different means, in order to prevent further destabilization of the region. The United States would rely on a broad spectrum of national power, primarily diplomatic, informational, and economic resources, to achieve its goals. While Indyk made clear that U.S. policy in Iraq was regime change, he was less specific regarding Iran, suggesting the policy would initially focus on modifying Iran's behavior. Dual Containment was

---

[68]Ansari, 135-137; Daniel, 232-233; Pollack, 259.

a defensive strategy designed to limit Iran's aggressive new foreign policy. A significant aspect

of this policy was to apply pressure on Europe and Japan to restrict trade with Iran (a new source

of economic growth that Iran relied upon). But the United States was unable to pressure Russia

and China to restrict arms sales to Iran, and unable to apply much pressure to Europe or Japan

while American corporations continued to purchase Iranian oil, and continued, at least

marginally, to do business with Iran. For instance, in 1992, American exports to Iran still totaled

almost $750 million annually.[69]

Israel was increasingly threatened by Iran's rhetoric and Hizbollah sponsored attacks

targeting Israeli diplomatic establishments. The Israeli government found an ally in the new

Republican controlled Congress, and immediately began lobbying for tougher sanctions against

Iran through the powerful American Israeli Public Affairs Committee (AIPAC). Soon,

Republicans in Congress recognized the administration's Iran policy was failing, and began to

implement a foreign policy of their own via economic sanctions. In 1993, Senator John McCain

introduced and Congress passed the Iran-Iraq Non-Proliferation Act. Then in January 1995,

Senator Alfonse D'Amato introduced legislation to ban all trade with Iran and prevent U.S.

corporations from purchasing Iranian oil. Yet despite the policy of Dual Containment, by 1995,

American exports to Iran had only dropped to just under $278 million dollars.[70]

---

[69]Hunter, *Iran's Foreign Policy in the Post-Soviet Era,* 50; Pollack, 261-264, 268; U.S. Census Bureau, "Foreign Trade in Goods with Iran—1992," http://www.census.gov/foreign-trade/balance/c5070.html#1992 (accessed March 1, 2013).

[70]Ansari, 143-145; Hunter, *Iran's Foreign Policy in the Post-Soviet Era*, 50-52; Trita Parsi, *Treacherous Alliance: The Secret Dealings of Israel, Iran, and the U.S.* (New Haven, Connecticut: Yale University Press, 2007), 183-187; Pollack, 269-271; U.S. Census Bureau, "Foreign Trade in Goods with Iran—1995," http://www.census.gov/foreign-trade/balance/c5070.html#1995 (accessed March 1, 2013).

Rafsanjani's Hail Mary: CONOCO

In 1995, Rafsanjani made one last effort to improve relations with the United States through a strategy of economic enticement to preempt containment. Rafsanjani knew several American corporations (e.g., Boeing, Microsoft, and Coca Cola) were publicly interested in expanding operations to Iran. In a bid to accelerate economic reengagement, Iran announced on March 6, 1995, that the American corporation CONOCO had won a $1 billion contract to develop two Iranian offshore oil fields. This decision, which would have required the approval of both Rafsanjani and Khamenei, surprised many in the United States and sparked a debate within Congress and the administration about the contract's legality. Although CONOCO had previously gained State Department approval for the bid, the potential deal threatened to undermine official U.S. policy towards Iran, and only intensified Israeli concerns that the United States was not holding Iran accountable for its actions.[71]

President Clinton quickly recognized that congressional interests threatened to dictate the terms of his Iran foreign policy, and that the CONOCO deal faced stiff opposition from AIPAC and a majority in Congress. So on March 15, 1995, the president signed Executive Order 12957, prohibiting any U.S. entity from engaging in transactions to develop Iranian petroleum resources, effectively canceling the CONOCO deal. Then on May 6, 1995, the president went even further, and signed Executive Order 12959, prohibiting all trade, financial, and commercial transactions with Iran. Finally, in late 1995, House Speaker Newt Gingrich prevailed in his not-so-subtle effort to appropriate $20 million for a CIA covert action program in Iran, while the House and Senate finally agreed on a final version of Senator D'Amato's bill, the Iran-Libya Sanctions Act

---

[71] Ansari, 141-142; Hunter, *Iran's Foreign Policy in the Post-Soviet Era*, 52; Pollack, 271-272.

(ILSA). Congress and the Israeli lobby had transformed Clinton's Dual Containment defensive strategy into a proactive policy approach towards Iran.[72]

In the face of comprehensive U.S. trade sanctions and public disclosure of the CIA's new $20 million covert action program targeting Iran, Khamenei and Iran's conservative hardliners were convinced the United States was still intent on regime change. From 1995 to 1996, Lebanese Hizbollah, HAMAS, and Palestinian Islamic Jihad escalated attacks targeting Israeli soldiers and civilians in southern Lebanon and northern Israel. Then on June 25, 1996, a large truck bomb detonated outside the Khobar Towers complex in Saudi Arabia, killing 19 and wounding 372 U.S. service members. A Saudi investigation tentatively identified the Hizbollah affiliate responsible, Hizbollah al-Hijaz, a Saudi-Shia revolutionary group formed two years earlier in Lebanon with the support of the IRGC. Although many in the Clinton administration suspected direct Iranian involvement, the intelligence was inconclusive. An infuriated President Clinton directed the Department of Defense to develop a range of military options targeting Iran in response, but recognizing that even a limited strike could escalate and lead to full scale war, the president opted instead for issuing a strong warning for Iran to prevent further acts of terrorism. Despite additional intelligence provided by the Saudis, and a June 2001 indictment in the Eastern District of Virginia charging 13 Saudis and one Lebanese man in the attack, the true source of the attack is still debated. In June 2007, former Secretary of Defense William Perry acknowledged in an interview, "I believe that the Khobar Tower bombing was probably masterminded by Osama bin Laden. I can't be sure of that, but in retrospect, that's what I believe.

---

[72]Hunter, *Iran's Foreign Policy in the Post-Soviet Era*, 52-53; U.S. Government Printing Office, Federal Register, vol. 60, no. 52, "Executive Order 12957 of March 15, 1995," http://www.gpo.gov/fdsys/pkg/FR-1995-03-17/pdf/95-6849.pdf (accessed February 10, 2013); Government Printing Office, Federal Register, vol. 60, no. 89, "Executive Order 12959 of May 6, 1995," http://www.gpo.gov/fdsys/pkg/FR-1995-05-09/pdf/95-11694.pdf (accessed February 10, 2013); James Risen, "Congress OKs House Plan to Fund Covert Action in Iran," *Los Angeles Times*, December 22, 1995, http://articles.latimes.com/1995-12-22/news/mn-16920_1_intelligence-budget (accessed March 1, 2013).

At the time, he was not a suspect. At the time…all of the evidence was pointing to Iran."[73]

Regardless of the true origins of the attack, Iran's belligerent behavior only served to strengthen

U.S. policy makers' resolve to further contain Iran. On August 5, 1996, the president signed the

Iran-Libya Sanctions Act (ILSA) into law, imposing economic sanctions on foreign entities with

investments in Iran's energy sector.[74]

Dialogue of Civilizations

Iran's 1997 presidential election was a contest between the conservative hardliners and a

new reformist-pragmatist coalition, personified by the intellectual cleric Mohammad Khatami.

Khatami campaigned on a populist platform advocating increased political freedom, civil rights,

and a moderate foreign policy. He surprised many Iranians and international observers, winning

69 percent of the electorate, almost 30 million votes. Khatami's victory also appeared to present a

genuine opportunity for Iranian political reform and rapprochement with the United States. His

victory shocked many conservatives, and initially empowered Khatami to make considerable

reforms. Khatami appointed a female vice president, and removed several long-serving regime

hardliners. He convinced Khamenei to dismiss the controversial commander of the IRGC, refused

to reappoint the infamous Ali Fallahian as the head of Iran's Ministry of Intelligence and Security

(MOIS), and replaced Ali Akbar Velayati, an active proponent of anti-Americanism, as foreign

minister.[75]

---

[73]UPI.com, "Perry: U.S. Eyed Iran Attack After Bombing," June 6, 2007, http://www.upi.com/Business_News/Security-Industry/2007/06/06/Perry-US-eyed-Iran-attack-after-bombing/UPI-70451181161509/ (accessed January 21, 2013).

[74]Hunter, *Iran's Foreign Policy in the Post-Soviet Era,* 53; Kenneth Katzman, "Congressional Research Service Report for Congress: The Iran-Libya Sanctions Act (ILSA)," http://www.dtic.mil/cgi-bin/GetTRDoc?AD=ADA475663 (accessed January 21, 2013); Pollack, 278-280; Wright, *The Iran Primer: Power, Politics, and U.S. Policy,* 140.

[75]Keddie, 269-270; Pollack, 312-315.

Khatami immediately announced his new approach to international relations based on

détente, or what he termed a *dialogue of civilizations*.[76] He was introduced to the American

public during a January 7, 1998 interview with Christiane Amanpour. During the interview, he

often spoke directly to the American public, expressing his regret about misperceptions,

miscommunication, and mutual distrust. Khatami compared the Iranian revolution to the

American revolution, and said, "I respect the American nation because of their great civilization."

He also stressed the importance of viewing U.S.-Iran relations "within their proper context and

with circumspection." Regarding the hostage situation, he stated,

> I do know that the feelings of the great American people have been hurt, and of course I
> regret it. Yet, these same feelings were also hurt when bodies of young Americans were
> brought back from Vietnam, but the American people never blamed the Vietnamese
> people…the feelings of our people were seriously hurt by U.S. policies. And as you said,
> in the heat of the revolutionary fervor, things happen which cannot be fully contained or
> judged according to usual norms.

Regarding the issue of rapprochement, Khatami responded, "Firstly, nothing should prevent

dialogue and understanding between two nations, especially between their scholars and thinkers.

Right now, I recommend the exchange of professors, writers, scholars, artists, journalists, and

tourists." Khatami reminded the American people of the causes of mutual distrust: the 1953 coup,

the capitulations, and American support of the shah. Yet each time he countered by suggesting

that both nations could and should move beyond previous policy errors. On the issue of support

for terrorism, Khatami explained, "If I learn of any instance of such assistance to terrorism, I shall

deal with it, so will our Leader, and so will our entire system. At the same time, supporting

peoples who fight for the liberation of their land is not, in my opinion, supporting terrorism."

Regarding Iran's opposition to the Middle East Peace Process, he clarified,

> We have declared our opposition to the peace process because we believe it will not
> succeed. At the same time, we have clearly said that we don't intend to impose our views
> on others or stand in their way. We seek a peace through which Jews, Muslims, and

---

[76]Hunter, *Iran's Foreign Policy in the Post-Soviet Era*, 54.

Christians, and indeed each and every Palestinian, could freely determine their own destiny. However, the impression of the people of the Middle East and Muslims in general is that certain foreign policy decisions of the U.S. are in fact made in Tel Aviv and not in Washington.[77]

Khatami's overtures faced initial skepticism by many U.S. policy makers still suspicious of Iranian overtures, so he sent informal, unofficial emissaries to the United States to meet with scholars, businesspeople, and government officials to discuss the possibilities of engagement. According to Kenneth Pollack, Director for Gulf affairs in the NSC from 1999-2001,

> I personally met with more than a dozen of Khatami's unofficial diplomats in various informal settings. They all came armed with a message and a mission. The message was that real change was taking place in Iran and Khatami and those around him wanted to explore the possibility of beginning a process of rapprochement. Their mission was to find out whether the Clinton administration was interested, and whether the United States would be willing and able to help Khatami to move down this path. Khatami was fighting a fierce internal battle for greater control over Iranian policy. If Khatami was going to make any progress, he needed the United States to demonstrate its goodwill in ways that the hardliners would find it impossible to dismiss.[78]

Clinton's Track Two Diplomacy

The Clinton administration responded with a type of track-two diplomacy, in the hope that positive U.S. gestures would serve to solidify Khatami's support and marginalize his opponents. In 1997, the administration relaxed visa restrictions to encourage more Iranian travel to the United States. That October, the administration sent an invitation through the Swiss Embassy's American Interest Section in Tehran to meet with high-level Clinton administration officials without preconditions, but they never received a response. That same month, in a move supported by many in Iran, the State Department added the MeK to its list of international terrorist organizations. The administration ended the embargo on Iranian pistachios and carpets, repealed many sanctions limiting the sale of food and medicine, and eventually allowed the sale

---

[77]CNN.com, "Transcript of Interview with Iranian President Mohammad Khatami," January 7, 1998, http://www.cnn.com/WORLD/9801/07/iran/interview.html (accessed February 5, 2013).

[78]Pollack, 317.

of Boeing aircraft parts to repair Iran's aging airliner fleet. In May 1998, Vice President Gore

requested the Saudi government mediate a direct dialogue between both nations, but Iran

countered that engagement should proceed slowly at first, particularly through academic and

economic exchanges. While the Clinton administration preferred a policy of direct diplomatic

engagement to normalize relations, Khatami recognized that more common ground was needed

before substantive negotiations could succeed.[79]

In a June 17, 1998 speech, Secretary of State Madeleine Albright assured Iranians,

> We are ready to explore further ways to build mutual confidence and avoid
> misunderstandings. The Islamic Republic should consider parallel steps. As the wall of
> mistrust comes down, we can develop with the Islamic Republic, when it is ready, a road
> map leading to normal relations.[80]

In a March 17, 2000 speech before the American-Iranian Council, Secretary Albright went further

than any previous administration in admitting previous American foreign policy errors,

specifically acknowledging America's role in the 1953 overthrow of Mossadeq, describing it as

"a setback for Iran's political development." She admitted, "The United States must bear its fair

share of responsibility for the problems that have arisen in U.S.-Iranian relations," and

acknowledged that, "After the election of President Khatami in 1997, we began to adjust the lens

through which we viewed Iran." [81] President Clinton also personally demonstrated his support for

Khatami, and in September 2000, after addressing the UN General Assembly, he took the

---

[79]Ansari, 157; U.S. Department of State, Office of the Coordinator for Counterterrorism, "Foreign Terrorist Organizations," October 8, 1997, http://www.state.gov/www/global/terrorism/terrorist_orgs_list.html (accessed March 20, 2013); Wright, *The Iran Primer: Power, Politics, and U.S. Policy*, 140.

[80]Federation of American Scientists, "Secretary of State Madeleine K. Albright Remarks at 1998 Asia Society Dinner," June 17, 1998, http://www.fas.org/news/iran/1998/980617a.html (accessed March 28, 2013).

[81]Federation of American Scientists, "Secretary of State Madeleine K. Albright Remarks before the American-Iranian Council," March 17, 2000, http://www.fas.org/news/iran/2000/000317.html (accessed March 28, 2013).

unprecedented step of staying to listen to President Khatami's remarks. Thus the stage was set, but the process of rapprochement and reengagement would be slow and steady.[82]

Iran's Conservatives Strike Back

While the Clinton administration did its best to ensure policy actions matched diplomatic rhetoric, Khatami worked hard to set the conditions for the normalization of international relations and implement his domestic program of liberal reform. During his first year, Khatami eased social and political restrictions. New media outlets vigorously supported his reformist agenda, and boldly criticized many influential conservatives within the government. But domestic reform, offers of dialogue with the United States, and media criticism convinced Khamenei and many of his conservative supporters that things had gone too far. When reformist candidates won a majority of seats in Iran's 1999 local council elections, particularly in Tehran, the conservatives decided to take matters into their own hands. Within the first 18 months of Khatami's presidency, nine reformist leaders were murdered or disappeared. After investigations identified that rogue elements within Iran's MOIS were responsible, Khamenei was forced to purge the organization of conservatives, and appointed moderate reformists in their place. But after conservatives in the judiciary shut down several reformist newspapers, thousands of students staged protests throughout 1998 and 1999. The conflict boiled over in 1999, in what came to be known as the Reformist Revolution. That May, four student leaders were arrested, and in July, the Majles passed a law limiting freedom of the press. After the judiciary ordered the closure of another reformist newspaper, students in Tehran clashed with regime security forces. Protests quickly spread to other cities, and after several students were killed and over 1,000 arrested, Khatami was forced to denounce the protests. Many felt betrayed by Khatami, who never intended to accomplish reform by violent means, but the actions of the radical reformists had compromised

[82]Wright, *The Iran Primer: Power, Politics, and U.S. Policy,* 141.

Khatami's agenda. Iran's hardliners were now convinced they could undermine Khatami's domestic reforms and efforts to reengage the United States. Despite this setback, however, the reformists fared well in the Sixth Majles elections of 2000, winning a strong majority. But Khatami and the reformists soon recognized that the Islamic establishment would do whatever was necessary to oppose any threat to the existing system. Conservative clerics rallied around Khamenei, as Supreme Leader, who was finally more powerful than Khatami, as president. Khamenei then simply used his control of the judiciary and Guardian Council to block most of the new Majles' reform legislation. By 2001, Iran's political system was held hostage to the standoff between the Khatami reformists and Khamenei conservatives. Khatami won reelection in June 2001 by an even wider margin than he did in 1997 (77 percent versus 69 percent), but his power and influence was greatly constrained by Khamenei's growing influence. It now appeared that Khatami's preferred gradual approach to rapprochement would take even more time to achieve results.[83]

Clinton: Analysis

Unfortunately, Rafsanjani's final effort to save Iran from itself in 1995 was destined to failure because of Iran's erratic foreign policy of the 1990s. Although the Clinton administration's Dual Containment policy was less punitive to Iran, House Republicans and the powerful Israeli lobby used legislation to send a clear message to regime hardliners and laid the groundwork for future crippling economic sanctions. Both sides were also constrained by politics, primarily internal conservative hardliners opposed to rapprochement. As Shireen Hunter observed,

---

[83]Ansari, 158; Daniel, 237-257; Mark J. Gasiorowski, "The Power Struggle in Iran," *Middle East Policy* 7, no. 4 (October 2000): 22-36; Katzman, 2; Hunter, *Iran's Foreign Policy in the Post-Soviet Era,* 54; Keddie, 275-278.

In short, both sides missed an opportunity to improve relations. Culprits were those elements in the U.S. foreign policy establishment determined to bring about regime change in Iran and Iranian factions that sacrificed Iran's national interests for their petty ambitions. Iran would come to regret this failure.[84]

The victory of Khatami and the reformists in 1997, however, presented the best opportunity yet for improved relations between the United States and Iran. History will likely show that the Clinton administration took appropriate steps to demonstrate its willingness to engage, but as Khatami recognized, the process would be slow, and required more common ground in order to dispel the mutual distrust of the previous two decades. This lack of common ground existed primarily because both nations still lacked formal diplomatic relations with the other. Iranian Foreign Minister Kamal Kharrazi later said in 2002, "I regret that Clinton failed to do better to finish the job. They had some efforts and took some positive positions but mixed those positions with some negative elements."[85] Although Khatami faced considerable internal resistance to his transformative agenda, the prospect of rapprochement was finally within reach. Ultimately, success would depend on both sides' ability, as Madeleine Albright said, to adjust the lens through which they viewed the other.

The dynamics of the global political economy at the end of the twentieth century forced Iran to pursue a more realist foreign policy than originally espoused by Khomeini, and this shift offered each successive American president with limited opportunities for rapprochement. Although each instance was unique, they all failed primarily due to the severance of diplomatic relations, which bred further misunderstanding and mutual distrust. For the United States, in the shadow of the Cold War, Iran foreign policy was never a priority, inadequately resourced and poorly coordinated. When policy decisions were made, it was typically done in crisis

---

[84] Hunter, *Iran's Foreign Policy in the Post-Soviet Era,* 56.

[85]Barbara Slavin, "Q&A with Iranian Foreign Minister Kamal Kharrazi," *USA Today,* September 18, 2002, http://usatoday30.usatoday.com/news/world/2002-09-18-iran-full-interview_x.htm (accessed March 1, 2013).

management mode, as opposed to developing a comprehensive approach to normalize relations. For Iran, Khomeini's Shia revolutionary ideology and the fragmented nature of Iran's political system prevented the Rafsanjani pragmatists and Khatami reformists from making substantive foreign policy reforms. On both sides, the issue of rapprochement also had significant domestic political implications and liabilities. Neither government was able to obtain a majority consensus to support rapprochement, and remained deeply divided along idealist versus realist perspectives.

For Iranians, the lessons of 1953 and 1979 combined with Rafsanjani's failed efforts to confirm their conviction that the Americans could not be trusted, and were still intent on undermining their revolution. For Americans, the lesson of 1979 and each successive failure at rapprochement convinced policy makers that the Iranians were duplicitous and could not be trusted. Both the Reagan and Bush administration efforts failed because rapprochement was never a policy goal, but a potential, however unlikely, side effect of Middle East crisis management policy decisions. Although the Clinton administration's track-two diplomacy with the Khatami reformists represented the best opportunity so far, Khatami first needed to garner enough domestic support to ensure the success of his dialogue of civilizations foreign policy. This process needed more time, at a minimum a decade, if not a generation, to erase the mutual trauma and distrust, and find common ground to move forward. Yet there were still many opposed to rapprochement on both sides. The root causes of this resistance were three issues on which both sides refused to compromise: Iran's position regarding Israel, nuclear proliferation, and Iran's support of terrorism abroad. Iranian hardline conservatives expressed their initial opposition in 1999, but it would be several years before American hardline conservatives would reveal their true intentions. As before, it would be up to the next administration to pick up where Clinton and Khatami left off.

MISSED OPPORTUNITY

Although Khatami's internal reforms and offers of détente provided hope for improved

bilateral relations, Iran was not an immediate priority for the George W. Bush administration, and

many senior administration officials had conflicting views on how to deal with Iran. Secretary of

State Colin Powell and National Security Advisor Condoleezza Rice were both realists in the

mold of former National Security Adviser Brent Scowcroft, who along with many in the

Department of State and NSC, wanted to continue the Clinton administration's efforts to

normalize relations with Iran. On the other side were the neoconservative idealists, or neocons as

they have since been labeled, led by Vice President Dick Cheney and Secretary of Defense

Donald Rumsfeld. Shaped by their Iran experiences in previous administrations, the neocons

opposed the Clinton administration's efforts at engagement, and instead preferred unilateral

efforts to affect regime change in Iraq, Syria, and Iran.[86]

By 2001, U.S.-Iran relations were mostly limited to the United Nations 6+2 Talks on

Afghanistan. Hosted by the UN, this forum included the six nations bordering Afghanistan, plus

the United States and Russia. The group focused on enforcement of an arms embargo on the

Taliban, counter-narcotics initiatives, and humanitarian relief efforts, but American lack of

interest and effort frustrated the Iranian delegation. Logically, Iran had a legitimate interest in

Afghanistan, and viewed the Taliban and al Qaeda as threats to regional stability. The NSC

initiated an Iran policy review in early 2001, but in the meantime the administration continued the

[86]Hunter, *Iran's Foreign Policy in the Post-Soviet Era,* 56-57; Steven Mufson, and Marc Kaufman, "Longtime Foes U.S., Iran Explore Improved Relations," *Washington Post*, October 29, 2001.

current policy of containment. On September 11, 2001, the Iran policy review was still ongoing; any Iran policy decision would now have to wait.[87]

U.S.-Iran Cooperation in Afghanistan

Iran's response to 9/11 surprised many observers: spontaneous candlelight vigils in Tehran mourned the American dead, the mayors of Tehran and Isfahan sent condolence messages to the people of New York City, and Iranians observed a moment of silence before a national soccer match. The Iranian government issued a strong statement condemning the terrorist attacks, and President Khatami publicly expressed his "deep regret and sympathy with the victims." During his November visit to the UN General Assembly, Khatami went so far as to request permission to visit ground zero in order to offer prayers and light a candle for the victims.[88]

After 9/11, Powell recognized that the crisis presented an opportunity to use international cooperation against al Qaeda as a platform to strengthen America's strategic relationship with Middle East regional powers, and in turn, use that momentum to solve the Israeli-Palestinian conflict. He instructed his staff to develop a comprehensive diplomatic strategy to support the war on terrorism. In response to Iran's sympathetic response, the administration sent a message via the Swiss Embassy in Tehran, thanking Iran for its support and requesting information about

[87]Ansari, 181; Stephen Carter, "Iran's Interest in Afghanistan and their Implications for NATO," *International Journal* (Autumn 2010): 982; Pollack, 344-346; Elaine Sciolino, "Iran Finds a Not-So-Great Satan on Its Doorstep," *New York Times*, September 20, 1998.

[88]CNN.com World Edition, "Attacks Draw Mixed Response in Mideast," September 12, 2001, http://www.archives.cnn.com/2001/WORLD/europe/09/12/mideast.reaction/index.htm (accessed March 10, 2013); Nazila Fathi, "A Nation Challenged: Tehran; Iran Softens Tone Against the United States," *New York Times*, September 21, 2001, http://www.newyorktimes.com/2001/09/21/world/a-nation-challenged-tehran-iran-softens-tone-against-the-united-states.html (accessed March 28, 2013); Alan Sipress and Steven Mufson, "U.S. Explores Recruiting Iran Into New Coalition," *Washington Post*, September 25, 2001; Barbara Slavin, "Khatami Worried About Afghan Quagmire for U.S.," *USA Today*, November 12, 2001, http://usatoday30.usatoday.com/news/attack/2001/11/12/khatami-usat.htm (accessed March 20, 2013); Time Magazine Photo Essay, "Tehran Candlelight Vigil." (September 18, 2001), www.time.com/time/europe/photoessays/vigil/2.html (accessed December 1, 2012).

Osama bin Laden and the Taliban. Khatami recognized this might be Iran's best opportunity yet to improve relations. He convinced Khamenei and the conservative hardliners that cooperation with the United States in Afghanistan was in Iran's best interest, and Khamenei authorized the Iranian government to consider possibilities for direct negotiations with the United States.[89] A senior Iranian diplomat later said,

> The general impression was (that 9/11) was a national tragedy for the United States and that success in addressing that national tragedy was extremely important for the U.S. public in general and the administration in particular…there was not another moment in U.S. history when there was more of a psychological need for success on the U.S. part. That is why we consciously decided not to qualify our cooperation on Afghanistan or make it contingent upon a change in U.S. policy, believing, erroneously, that the impact would be of such magnitude that it would automatically have altered the nature of Iran-U.S. relations."[90]

In mid-October, several members of congress, led by Senator Arlen Specter, hosted Iran's UN ambassador, Hadi Nejad Hosseinian, at a private dinner on Capitol Hill to discuss U.S.-Iran cooperation. An Iranian official, commenting on the dinner, observed "many things have been done by Iran in a very deliberate and policy oriented way. We look forward to continuing the positive atmosphere and to seeing some modification of U.S. policy in Iran."[91] U.S.-Iran cooperation on Afghanistan progressed quickly, and many on both sides hoped this would expand to broader discussions. Cooperation was facilitated primarily through the UN 6+2 venue, led by the Bush administration's Special Envoy for Afghanistan, Ambassador James Dobbins. Iran leveraged its influence with the Northern Alliance to gain their initial support of coalition military operations, agreed to allow American humanitarian relief supplies to be

---

[89]Flynt Leverett, "Illusion and Reality," *The American Prospect* (September 2006), http://newamerica.net/publications/articles/2006/illusion_and_reality (accessed March 10, 2013); PBS Frontline, "Terror and Tehran: Does America's war on terror hold democracy hostage in Iran?" http://www.pbs.org/wgbh/pages/frontline/shows/tehran/ (accessed March 1, 2013); Sipress and Mufson.

[90]Barbara Slavin, "A Broken Engagement," *The National Interest*, no. 92 (November/December 2007): 39.

[91]Mufson and Kaufman.

unloaded at Iranian ports and trucked into southwestern Afghanistan, and offered to conduct

search and rescue missions for downed American pilots over Iranian territory. Remarkably, Iran

provided the United States with critical targeting information regarding Taliban positions, and

offered to allow American transport aircraft to stage at eastern Iranian airstrips to assist

operations in western Afghanistan. During the UN 6+2 Foreign Ministers Conference in

November, Iranian Foreign Minister Kamal Kharrazi passed Secretary Powell a message that

read, "the United States should know that the Iranian people and the Iranian government stand

with the United States in its time of need and absolutely condemn these vicious terrorist

attacks."[92] After the meeting, Powell and Kharrazzi briefly met and shook hands in what many

felt was the most positive diplomatic message between both nations since 1979.[93]

After the Taliban was defeated, the UN hosted the International Conference on

Afghanistan, in Bonn, Germany from November through December 2001, to develop a new

Afghan government and select an interim leader. James Dobbins represented the United States

during the proceedings, and enjoyed a close working relationship with his Iranian counterpart,

Deputy Foreign Minister Javad Zarif. According to Dobbins' 2007 congressional testimony,

Iran's cooperation was crucial to the success of the conference. The Iranian delegation insisted on

including language in Afghanistan's new constitution committing the Afghan government to

democratic elections and combating international terrorism. Towards the end of the conference,

Iran used its influence over the Northern Alliance delegation to prevent an internal Afghan

---

[92]Slavin, "A Broken Engagement," 39.

[93]Mufson and Kaufman; Parsi, *Treacherous Alliance,* 227; Pollack, 346; PBS Frontline, "Terror and Tehran; Slavin, "A Broken Engagement," 39; U.S. Congress. House, Committee on Government Oversight and Reform, "U.S. Diplomacy With Iran: The Limits of Tactical Engagement." Testimony of Hillary Mann before the Subcommittee on National Security and Foreign Affairs. 110th Cong., 1st sess., November 7, 2007, http://democrats.oversight.house.gov/images/stories/subcommittees/NS_Subcommittee/11.7.07_Iran_II/HillaryMannLeveretttestimony 1107.pdf (accessed March 1, 2013).

dispute, which resulted in the formation of the new transitional government. Iran further sent a signal by sending the most senior delegation to Karzai's inauguration, and Iranian Foreign Minister Kamal Kharrazi personally ensured that troublesome Afghan warlord Ismael Khan attended the ceremony in support of Karzai and the new government.[94]

At the January 2002 Afghanistan Donors Conference in Tokyo, Iran pledged $540 million in assistance for the new Afghan government, compared to the $290 million committed by the United States. While in Tokyo, an Iranian representative approached Dobbins and expressed his desire to not only continue cooperation in Afghanistan, but work on other issues with the appropriate American officials. At this same conference, Treasury Secretary Paul O'Neill received a similar message from the Iranian government. Both Dobbins and O'Neill reported Iran's offers to Rice and Powell, but no reply was given to Iran. Later, during a March 2002 meeting in Geneva, the Iranian delegation met again with Dobbins, and offered military assistance to house and train up to 20,000 Afghan troops under the American led effort. Dobbins relayed this offer to the administration, but Powell deferred the issue to Rice, who deferred the issue to Rumsfeld. Days later, the issue was on the agenda for discussion at a NSC Principals Committee meeting. During the meeting, Dobbins relayed Iran's offer, but Rumsfeld ignored the issue, and no one else seemed interested. The discussion moved on, and no response was given to Iran.[95] It now appears that throughout late 2001 and early 2002, the neocons within the administration were already looking for reasons not to cooperate and engage with Iran.

---

[94] James Dobbins, "Negotiating with Iran: Reflections from Personal Experience," *The Washington Quarterly* (January 2010): 149-154; James Dobbins, "Negotiating with Iran," Testimony presented before the House Committee on Oversight and Government Reform, Subcommittee on National Security and Foreign Affairs on November 7, 2007, http://www.rand.org/pubs/testimonies/CT293.html (accessed March 1, 2013); Parsi, *Treacherous Alliance,* 227-229.

[95] Dobbins, "Negotiating with Iran: Reflections from Personal Experience," 155.

After the Bonn Conference, the decision was made to continue the direct dialogue between the United States and Iran on Afghanistan through a separate channel of discreet, monthly meetings in Europe. This venue became known as the Geneva Contact Group. James Dobbins, Ambassador Ryan Crocker and Hillary Mann (NSC Director for Iran and Afghanistan Policy) were the first senior U.S. officials to participate in these discussions. According to Mann's 2007 Congressional testimony, the United States provided Iran with intelligence regarding suspected al Qaeda operatives who fled Afghanistan for Iran. Iran arrested many of these individuals, provided the United States with copies of their passports, and allowed U.S. interrogators to question some of the prisoners before deporting them. Iran's navy even cooperated with the American led interdiction fleet in the Persian Gulf, sharing intelligence regarding Iraqi illicit oil smuggling. In response, State Department officials considered possible incentives to reward Tehran for its cooperation, including the possibility of expanding the Clinton administration's previous decision to lift sanctions on select Iranian exports.[96]

Then in January, the Iranian delegates communicated their government's approval to broaden discussions beyond Afghanistan. According to Dobbins, "It was consistent with their behavior that they wanted strategic talks."[97] Although many in the administration did not appear to recognize it at the time, U.S. diplomats had finally accomplished what no administration since 1979 had been able to achieve: direct, face-to-face meetings on a matter of mutual interest, with Iranian diplomats permitted to discuss multiple topics. Secretary Powell alluded to this accomplishment during a December 9th interview:

---

[96]CBS News, "Iran Gave U.S. Help On Al Qaeda After 9/11," September 4, 2009, http://www.cbsnews.com/2102-202_162-4508360.html?tag=contentMain;contentBody (accessed March 12, 2013); Alan Sipress, "Bush's Speech Shuts Door on Tenuous Opening to Iran," *Washington Post*, February 4, 2002; U.S. Congress.

[97]Parsi, *Treacherous Alliance,* 230.

We have been in discussions with the Iranians on a variety of levels and in some new ways since September 11th. Jim Dobbins spoke with Iranians in Bonn as we put together the new interim administration in Afghanistan, and I had a brief handshake and discussion with the Iranian prime minister in the UN. So there are a number of things going on and we recognize the nature of that regime and we recognize that the Iranian people are starting to try to find a new way forward and we are open to exploring new opportunities without having any vaseline in our eyes with respect to the nature of the government or the history of the past 22 years.[98]

Despite this tremendous breakthrough, however, some in the administration had already made up their minds regarding Iran policy. According to James Dobbins, "I saw no glimmer of interest outside of State" for entertaining the possibility of rapprochement with Iran.[99]

Behind the Scenes: Origins of the Bush Doctrine:

Despite the fact that the Bush administration had yet to develop an official Iran policy by 9/11, the events of that day ultimately provided the administration's neocons the justification they needed to pursue a unilateral, transformative foreign policy throughout the Middle East. Throughout the fall of 2001, although many in the White House and Pentagon quietly opposed any effort at rapprochement with the Iranian government, they tolerated the State Department's Geneva dialogue for its short-term benefits: the meetings facilitated the war in Afghanistan and the pending war plans for Iraq. Behind the scenes, however, a fierce battle ensued over Iran policy between the realists, who preferred dialogue and engagement, and the neocons, who favored regime change. The realists were based within the State Department, led by Secretary Powell, Deputy Secretary of State Richard Armitage, and Powell's Chief of Staff, Lawrence Wilkerson, but also included some within the NSC. The neocons in the Office of the Secretary of Defense (OSD) and NSC were led by Vice President Cheney, Secretary Rumsfeld, Deputy

---

[98]U.S. Department of State Archive (2001-2009), "Press Briefing on Board Plane En Route Moscow," December 9, 2001, http://2001-2009.state.gov/secretary/former/powell/remarks/2001/dec/6759.htm (accessed March 1, 2013).

[99]Parsi, *Treacherous Alliance,* 230.

Secretary of Defense Paul Wolfowitz, Under Secretary of Defense for Policy Douglas Feith, Secretary of State for Arms Control John Bolton, and Elliott Abrams. Condoleeza Rice and President Bush initially appeared to be somewhere in the middle. Powell, Armitage, and Wilkerson were trying to build a policy of engagement with Iran, but faced ferocious opposition from Cheney, Rumsfeld, and Wolfowitz.[100] According to Wilkerson, "Cheney and Rumsfeld were always there to sabotage our cooperation [with Iran] in Afghanistan if it got too far."[101]

The foundations of the global war on terror strategy, and what would become the Bush Doctrine, were immediately evident in President Bush's September 20, 2001 address to a joint session of Congress, when he said,

> We will pursue nations that provide aid or safe haven to terrorism. Every nation in every region now has a decision to make: either you are with us or you are with the terrorists. From this day forward, any nation that continues to harbor or support terrorism will be regarded by the United States as a hostile regime.[102]

Although the president did not call out Iran by name, the implications of this statement would influence the administration's Middle East policy discussions for the next 18 months.

As early as September 2000, a group of prominent neocon thinkers, led by Bill Kristol's Project for the New American Century, summarized their global strategy for the United States in a paper entitled "Rebuilding Americas Defenses," which argued the United States should be more assertive in the Middle East. On the same day of the president's address, this group of neocons sent an open letter to President Bush, encouraging him to expand the war on terror beyond al Qaeda, and recommending,

---

[100]Hunter, *Iran's Foreign Policy in the Post-Soviet Era*, 56-57; Parsi, *Treacherous Alliance*, 227-228; Pollack, 346-350; Barbara Slavin, *Bitter Friends, Bosom Enemies: Iran, the U.S., and the Twisted Path to Confrontation* (New York: St. Martin's Press, 2007), 196.

[101]Parsi, *Treacherous Alliance,* 228.

[102]Washington Post, "Text of President Bush's Address to a Joint Session of Congress and the Nation," September 20, 2011, http://www.washingtonpost.com/wpsrv/nation/specials/ attacked/ transcripts/bushaddress_092001.html (accessed January 29, 2013).

We believe the administration should demand that Iran and Syria immediately cease all military, financial, and political support for Hezbollah and its operations. Should Iran and Syria refuse to comply, the administration should consider appropriate measures of retaliation against these known state sponsors of terrorism.[103]

Many prominent neocons, including Bill Kristol, Eliot Cohen, Donald Kagan, Robert Kagan, Charles Krauthammer, and Richard Perle, signed the letter.

Days later, Secretary Rumsfeld first articulated his strategy for the campaign against terrorism in a short memorandum for the president entitled "Strategic Thoughts." This document, drafted by Douglas Feith and edited by Wolfowitz and Rumsfeld, was sent to President Bush for approval on September 30th. The paper, which would serve as a precursor for a strategic guidance document for the entire Department of Defense, summarized that "the U.S. strategic theme should be aiding local peoples to rid themselves of terrorists and to free themselves of regimes that support terrorism."[104]

In October 2001, Flynt Leverett, Middle East expert for the Department of State's Policy Planning Staff, was responsible for developing a strategy to address the offers of support from Syria, Libya, Iran, and other troublesome countries. Leverett's proposal to Powell was basically a quid pro quo engagement: if these countries agree to expel terrorist groups and cease efforts to acquire weapons of mass destruction, the United States, in return, will normalize relations. In December, when this policy proposal came up for discussion at a NSC Deputies Committee meeting (chaired by Deputy National Security Advisor Stephen Hadley), Hadley, as well as the representatives from the vice president's office and the OSD, rejected the idea. After the meeting,

---

[103]Hunter, *Iran's Foreign Policy in the Post-Soviet Era*, 57; Parsi, *Treacherous Alliance*, 227; Project for the New American Century, "Open Letter to President George W. Bush," September 20, 2001, http://www.newamericancentury.org/RebuildingAmericasDefenses.pdf (accessed February 6, 2013).

[104]Douglas J. Feith, *War and Decision: Inside the Pentagon at the Dawn of the War on Terrorism* (New York: HarperCollins, 2009), 81; Donald Rumsfeld, *Known and Unknown: A Memoir* (New York: Penguin Group, 2011), 373.

Hadley circulated the administration's position via memorandum, which stated, "If a state like Syria or Iran offers specific assistance, we will take it without offering anything in return. We will accept it without strings or promises."[105]

The Pentagon was already exploring options for regime change in Tehran. During the December 2001 Bonn Conference, two OSD employees assigned to the American delegation left during the negotiations to attend a secret meeting in Rome with an Iranian opposition group, set up by pro-Israel neocon Michael Ledeen. At the meeting, Larry Franklin and Harold Rhode, both from Douglas Feith's Office of Special Plans, offered to finance efforts to overthrow the Iranian government. Astonishingly, the Iranian dissident they met with was the same rogue operative responsible for the messy Iran-Contra affair, Manucher Ghorbanifar. The meeting was conducted without the knowledge or approval of the U.S. Ambassador or the CIA's Chief of Station. A second meeting took place in June 2002, but after CIA Director George Tenet and Secretary Powell discovered the Pentagon's plan, the meetings stopped and funds for the opposition groups was blocked.[106]

A Perfect Storm: the *Karine-A*

Israel and Pakistan were also alarmed about the increased cooperation between Iran and the United States. Pakistan was primarily interested in maintaining its influence in Afghanistan via its liaison relationship with the U.S. military and intelligence community, but Israel felt particularly threatened by this warming of relations. On September 21, 2001, Israeli Foreign

---

[105]John H. Richardson, "The Secret History of the Impending War with Iran That the White House Doesn't Want You to Know," *Esquire Magazine* (October 18, 2007), http://www.esquire.com/features/iranbriefing1107 (accessed March 1, 2013).

[106]Dobbins, "Negotiating with Iran: Reflections from Personal Experience," 157; Joshua Micah Marshall, Laura Rozen, and Paul Glastris, "Iran-Contra II?" *The Washington Monthly*, (October 2004), 16-17; Parsi, *Treacherous Alliance*, 231-233; George Tenet, *At the Center of the Storm: My Years at the CIA* (New York: Harper Collins, 2007), 313-315.

Minister Benjamin Netanyahu warned U.S. officials that Israel specifically opposed "any signs of U.S. cuddling up to Iran."[107] But when President Bush issued Executive Order 13224 on September 23rd, the Israelis were alarmed that HAMAS and Hizbollah were not on the administrations list of terrorist organizations.[108] Then in early October, reports surfaced in the media that the administration was planning a comprehensive Middle East peace initiative, which included support for a Palestinian state. As the president explained, "The idea of a Palestinian state has always been a part of a vision, so long as the right of Israel to exist is respected."[109] But Prime Minister Ariel Sharon and Foreign Minister Benjamin Netanyahu called this new approach a reward for terrorism. On October 24th, an Israeli government delegation met with John Bolton and provided intelligence that revealed Iran was progressing with a nuclear program, aided by Russia. The intelligence indicated Iran had built underground production facilities and purchased highly specialized aluminum and steel products (required for centrifuges) through two Russian companies.[110]

In late December and early January, reports from Afghanistan indicated the Afghan-Iran border was a high traffic area: IRGC and MOIS agents were infiltrating into western Afghanistan, while al Qaeda and Taliban leaders were fleeing into eastern Iran. Zalmay Khalilzad, the administration's new Special Envoy to Afghanistan, also reported that Iranian trained Afghan fighters were joined in western Afghanistan by IRGC units, who were providing financial and

---

[107]Hunter, *Iran's Foreign Policy in the Post-Soviet Era*, 59.

[108]Hunter, *Iran's Foreign Policy in the Post-Soviet Era*, 59; U.S. Department of State, Office of the Coordinator for Counterterrorism, "Executive Order 13224," September 23, 2001, http://www.state.gov/j/ct/ris/other/des/122570.htm (accessed January 30, 2013).

[109]Roger Hardy, "Bush 'endorses' Palestinian state," *BBC News*, Middle East Online Edition, October 2, 2001, http://news.bbc.co.uk/2/hi/middle_east/1575090.stm (accessed January 30, 2013).

[110]Seymour M. Hersh, "The Iran Game," *The New Yorker*, 77, iss. 38 (December 3, 2011): 42.

military support to create an Iranian sphere of influence. Although the issue of al Qaeda and

Taliban fighters fleeing into Iran was being addressed through the Geneva Contact Group (and

Iran was taking action), the reality was that the Afghan-Iran border was a 560 mile frontier

similar to the Afghan-Pakistan border tribal area. The region was sparsely populated and difficult

to govern: on the Iranian side, ethnic Pashtun and Baluchi tribes had historically resisted

government control, and engaged in guerilla warfare against Iran's security services. Those

security services, particularly the IRGC and MOIS, had traditionally exerted influence in western

Afghanistan, primarily in the region surrounding Herat, and maintained close ties with tribal

leaders and local warlords.[111]

This is where the reality of Iran's political system began to impact the Geneva dialogue.

Despite American requests for Iran to secure the border and detain each al Qaeda and Taliban

fighter in eastern Iran, it was an impossible task. Further complicating matters, local commanders

or conservative government officials, opposed to cooperating with the Americans, likely ignored

these requests. The Geneva dialogue with the reformists in Iran's foreign ministry could only do

so much, but to the neocons in the NSC and OSD, it appeared that Iran was now harboring

terrorists. Faced with reports of Iranian intelligence and security services operating in

Afghanistan, and what appeared to be complicity in allowing al Qaeda and Taliban suspects

refuge inside Iran, many administration officials complained that Iran was directly undermining

American efforts in Afghanistan. Only later would the administration acknowledge that most al

Qaeda and Taliban leadership and fighters had fled in the opposite direction: to the Spin Ghar and

Shahi-Kot eastern Afghan approaches to Pakistan's northwest tribal area.[112]

---

[111]BBC News, Middle East Online Edition, "Iranian Commanders Assassinated," October 18, 2009, http://news.bbc.co.uk/2/hi/middle_east/8312964.stm (accessed January 31, 2013); John Daniszewski, "Iran's Own Desert Storm," *Los Angeles Times*, March 21, 2000; Pollack, 347-349; Sipress, "Bush's Speech Shuts Door on Tenuous Opening to Iran."

[112]Hunter, *Iran's Foreign Policy in the Post-Soviet Era*, 59.

Then, as is always the case when dealing with Iran, someone in the regime went rogue.

On January 3, 2002, the Israel intercepted a Gaza bound ship, the *Karine-A*, while transiting the

Red Sea. On board, Israeli commandos discovered 50 tons of advanced weaponry, and the crew

admitted that the weapons were loaded off the coast of Iran. The operation was reportedly

orchestrated by Imad Mughniyah, the same member of Lebanese Hizbollah responsible for the

1985 hijacking of TWA flight 847, and the kidnapping of Americans in Lebanon during the

1980s. The timing, to say the least, was not propitious for the Geneva dialogue. The Israelis

immediately exploited the incident in an effort to derail support for a Palestinian state and

rapprochement with Iran. After reviewing the evidence, President Bush, Cheney, and Powell all

publicly condemned the incident. Both Arafat and the Iranian government denied the

connection.[113] Iranian Foreign Minister Kamal Kharrazi later said, "The *Karine-A* story was never

substantiated. If there is any trace that can substantiate the loading of this ship in an Iranian port,

we will follow it to the end. But we never received such information. I imagine this is a plot

fabricated by Israel."[114]

Although some observers suggested the Israelis were behind the entire affair, it is more

likely the incident can be attributed to conservative, hardline elements within the regime intent on

undermining Khatami's efforts at all costs. Interestingly, after the *Karine-A* incident, while James

Dobbins was meeting with his Iranian counterpart in Tokyo, he explained how events like the

------

[113]Hunter, *Iran's Foreign Policy in the Post-Soviet Era*, 59-60; Israel Ministry of Foreign Affairs, "Seizing of the Palestinian Weapons Ship Karine A," January 4, 2002, http://www.mfa.gov.il/MFA/Government/Communiques/2002/Seizing %20of%20the%20Palestinian%20weapons%20ship%20Karine%20A%20-.html (accessed July 26, 2012); Israel Ministry of Foreign Affairs, "Statement by IDF Chief-of-Staff Lt.-Gen. Shaul Mofaz regarding interception of ship Karine A," January 4, 2002, http:www.mfa.gov.il/MFA/ Government/Speeches+by+Israeli+leaders/2002/Statement+by+IDF+Chief-of-Staff+Lt-Gen+Shaul+Mofaz.html (accessed July 26, 2012); Matt Rees, Massimo Calabresi, Jamil Hamad and Aharon Klein, "Postmarked Tehran," *Time*, 159, iss. 3 (January 21, 2002): 54; Richardson.

[114]Slavin, "Q&A with Iranian Foreign Minister Kamal Kharrazi."

Karine-A affair represented an obstacle to cooperation. The Iranian diplomat acknowledged his

concerns, and replied,

> President Khatami met earlier this week with his National Security Council. He asked
> whether any of the agency heads present knew about this shipment. All of them denied
> any knowledge. If your government has information on the origin of these weapons that it
> can provide us, that would be most helpful."[115]

Of course, this was part of the message that Dobbins subsequently delivered to the administration,

but the message was ignored. Further, as has been demonstrated on numerous occasions, radical

elements within Iran's government that support Hizbollah and HAMAS do not necessarily

operate under the authority of the highest levels of the Iranian government, a distinction that

many in Washington refused to notice.

According to Lawrence Wilkerson, the *Karine-A* incident was a clear setback for Powell

within the administration. In an interview with Trita Parsi, Wilkerson said, "It put Powell back on

his heel about what was possible to achieve with the Iranians."[116] The *Karine-A* incident only

made the argument for engagement more difficult. The reality was most policy makers in the

administration were preoccupied with reconstruction and counterterrorism operations in

Afghanistan, while preparing the diplomatic case for invading Iraq. The sudden victory in

Afghanistan demonstrated the advantages of neocon foreign policy, and reinforced the belief of

many in the administration that preemptive, unilateral action was justified; in their opinion, the

United States did not need Iran. Armed with the recent Israeli intelligence suggesting Iran was

pursuing nuclear weapons and supporting international terrorism (via HAMAS and Hizbollah),

and reports from Afghanistan that Iran was harboring Taliban and al Qaeda terrorists, the neocons

finally had the evidence they needed to win the Iran policy debate.

---

[115]Dobbins, "Negotiating with Iran: Reflections from Personal Experience," 155.

[116]Parsi, *Treacherous Alliance*, 234.

<u>The Axis of Evil</u>

If President Bush had still not decided on a specific Iran policy by late January 2002, his State of the Union address on January 29, 2002 made the decision for him. In what is likely one of the worst foreign policy messaging blunders in American history, President Bush, in just four sentences, nearly sabotaged what, to date, had been America's greatest opportunity yet for improved relations with Iran since 1979. The president said,

> Our second goal is to prevent regimes that sponsor terror from threatening America or our friends and allies with weapons of mass destruction. Some of these regimes have been pretty quiet since September 11th, but we know their true nature. North Korea is a regime arming with missiles and weapons of mass destruction, while starving its citizens. Iran aggressively pursues these weapons and exports terror, while an unelected few repress the Iranian people's hope for freedom. Iraq continues to flaunt its hostility toward America and to support terror. The Iraqi regime has plotted to develop anthrax and nerve gas and nuclear weapons for over a decade…States like these, and their terrorist allies, constitute an axis of evil, arming to threaten the peace of the world.[117]

In what was supposed to be a narrative on the ongoing campaign against al Qaeda, and a preliminary justification for military intervention in Iraq, the president arbitrarily grouped Iran, Iraq, and North Korea together as the greatest threats to peace in the world. Despite the fact that neither country coordinated their foreign policy with the others, and were never connected to al Qaeda or the 9/11 attacks, this theme of a tripartite conspiracy provided the neocon justification for the preemptive, unilateral strategy that became the foundation of the Bush Doctrine.

The reality, however, is that the phrase *axis of evil* was a conveniently borrowed theme from World War II. In late 2001, David Frum, Special Assistant to the President for economic speechwriting, was tasked with articulating in just a few sentences the justification for invading Iraq. In the shadow of 9/11, Frum wanted to make a symbolic statement, in the likes of Churchill or FDR, to galvanize American public opinion. In notes attached to his recommended remarks

---

[117]Washington Post, "Text of President Bush's 2002 State of the Union Address," January 29, 2002, http://www.washingtonpost.com/wp-srv/onpolitics/transcripts/sou012902.htm (accessed January 30, 2013).

sent to senior Bush aide Michael Gerson, Frum compared al Qaeda, Hizbollah, Iran, and Iraq to the Tokyo-Rome-Berlin Axis powers. Frum's initial *axis of hatred* description of Iraq, Iran, and their terror proxies was embraced by Hadley and Rice, but changed to axis of evil by more senior administration officials in an effort to delineate the administration's theological justification for war. North Korea was added at the last minute; the consensus was that North Korea was also a rogue dictatorship, and three is always better than two. There is debate, however, about how well this statement was staffed within the administration. The *Wall Street Journal* reported in 2003 that some State Department officials only learned about the axis of evil language on the day of the speech, and despite efforts to tone down the rhetoric, were overruled by the administration.[118] Secretary Powell's response was, "These are the president's views. It's his speech, so salute and follow," according to a State Department official.[119] In his memoir, Frum is unabashedly pro-Israel, opposed to a two state solution on the grounds that it rewards terrorism, and dismissive of "foreign policy bureaucrats" in the State Department and CIA who were "eager to appease the Arab oil states."[120] In the end, the administration's Iran policy coalesced around grandiose prose penned by a relatively unknown Canadian journalist, who self-admittedly was not suited for the job of presidential speechwriter, had no experience in foreign policy, and who blamed the 9/11 attacks on "Middle East soft-liners" who "ran American foreign policy from February 1991 until September 2001."[121]

----

[118]David Frum, *The Right Man: An Inside Account of the Bush White House* (Westminster, MD: Random House, 2003), 234-238; Hendrick Hertzberg, "Axis Praxis," *The New Yorker*, January 13, 2003, http://www.newyorker.com/archive/2003/01/13/030113ta_ talk_hertzberg?printable=true (accessed January 29, 2013); Jay Solomon and David S. Cloud, "A Globe Journal Report: U.S.-Seoul Gap Feeds Korea Crisis," *Wall Street Journal*, January 2, 2003.

[119]Solomon and Cloud.

[120]Frum, 254.

[121]Ibid., 4, 294.

Immediately following the speech, the administration closed ranks on the neocon Iran position. On January 31st, Condoleeza Rice said, "Iran's direct support of regional and global terrorism, and its aggressive efforts to acquire weapons of mass destruction, belie any good intentions it displayed in the days after the world's worst terrorist attacks in history."[122] The following Sunday, Secretary Rumsfeld appeared on ABC's *This Week* claiming, "There isn't any doubt in my mind that the porous border between Iran and Afghanistan has been used for al-Qaida and Taliban to move into Iran and find refuge." He also said,

> The Iranians have not done what the Pakistan government has done—put troops along the border to prevent terrorists from escaping out of Afghanistan into their country. We have any number of reports that Iran has been permissive and allowed transit through their country of al-Qaida.[123]

Rice also appeared on CNN and said, "This regime (Iran) deserved to be on the list and this regime knows it deserved to be on the list." She also expressed concern about "Iranian attempts to surreptitiously influence Afghan politics at a very delicate time."[124] The administration's hubris was growing. When asked if the United States was planning a response to Iranian actions, Rumsfeld said, "We don't announce things we're going to do before we do them."[125] Secretary Powell then tried to tone down the rhetoric, saying, "We prefer diplomatic ways, political solutions. We're not looking for a war; we're trying to avoid war."[126]

In the midst of the administration's media barrage, Iranian Foreign Minister Kamal Kharrazi argued that Iran was doing its best to patrol the 560 mile border with Afghanistan, and pledged to deport any al Qaeda or Taliban members hiding in Iran. He further suggested, "Instead

---

[122]Sipress, "Bush's Speech Shuts Door on Tenuous Opening to Iran."

[123]Matt Kelley, "Iran Has Allowed Taliban, al-Qaida Members to Escape, Rumsfeld Says," Associated Press, February 3, 2002, http://www2.ljworld.com/news/2002/feb/03/iran_has_allowed/ (accessed January 30, 2013).

[124]Ibid.

[125]Ibid.

[126]Ibid.

of waging negative propaganda, the Americans had better give us any information they have so that we can go after (the terrorists)."[127] In response to Rumsfeld's veiled threat of a military response, Iran Foreign Ministry spokesman Hamid Reza Asefi replied, "I don't think America will make an irreparable mistake, the world public opinion would not allow it."[128] Ironically, the same Iranian government ministry supportive of the Geneva dialogue was now forced to counter American accusations and threats of military action. Foreign Minister Kharrazi later said,

> It was very strange for us and shocked everyone why Americans after all this cooperation in Afghanistan come up with this notion of the 'axis of evil.' Everyone was shocked. The story of al Qaeda as an excuse was not founded. It was very natural with the long border we have with Afghanistan and Pakistan and after removal of the Taliban, it was very natural for them to look for safe haven. But as soon as we found them, we have arrested them and sent them back to the countries of their origin. There have been many cases.[129]

Martin Indyk, former Assistant Secretary of State and author of the Dual Containment policy, summed it up best when he admitted, "I'd be surprised if the Iranians are quick to jump back into bed again."[130]

The speech was devastating for Khatami's reform movement, and it threatened to make him a lame duck president in only the first year of his second administration. Ali Ansari described the reaction in Iran:

> Few Iranians could reconcile themselves with the notion that they belonged in the same category as their old foe Saddam Hussein or the totalitarian regime in North Korea. More crucially, however, was the impact that the speech had on Khatami's own credibility. When he made the argument for Iranian support for coalition efforts in Afghanistan, he had stressed, in the face of concerted hardline opposition, that the potential rewards would be worth it.[131]

---

[127]Barbara Slavin, "Iran Seeks Help in Finding al-Qaeda, Taliban Fugitives," *USA Today*, February 6, 2002.

[128]Afshin Valinejad, "Iran Says a U.S. Attack on it Would be an 'Irreparable Mistake,'" *Associated Press*, February 4, 2002.

[129] Slavin, "Q&A with Iranian Foreign Minister Kamal Kharrazi."

[130]Sipress, "Bush's Speech Shuts Door on Tenuous Opening to Iran."

[131]Ansari, 186-187.

Iran's conservative hard-liners, however, were ecstatic. Until now, even some pragmatic conservatives (including Khamenei) had been willing to explore the possibility of rapprochement with the United States, but the axis of evil label only reinforced their convictions that nothing could be gained through dialogue. Seyyed Mohammad Kazem Sajjad-Pour, Director of Tehran's Institute for Political and International Studies, observed,

> Despite the fact that the perpetrators of the September 11th attacks were citizens of Saudi Arabia, Egypt and the UAE, and despite the fact that the Taliban were nurtured by the Pakistani military, it was Iran that Washington branded as one of the greatest supporters of international terrorism. The shift in Washington's stance bolstered the already existing perception of U.S. unreliability in any possible Iran-U.S. dialogue.[132]

Khatami's reformist movement was now clearly on the defensive, and the conservatives were now emboldened to adamantly oppose further reforms. The Bush administration's refusal to fully engage those elements of the Iranian government interested in negotiation only accelerated the hardliner's victory, and the consequence was a steady, irreversible deterioration of relations over the next 18 months.

In response to the State of the Union address, Iran refused to allow its delegation to attend the February Geneva Contact Group meeting. Although Khatami and the reformists were down, they were not finished. Amazingly, the Iranian delegation returned to the Geneva talks in March. According to Hillary Mann, "They said they had put their necks out to talk to us and they were taking big risks with their careers and their families and their lives."[133] The secret Geneva negotiations continued throughout 2002, but the dynamic of the meetings changed as U.S. policy shifted towards the issue of Iraq. Zalmay Khalilzad, recently appointed Special Envoy for Afghanistan, led the American delegation. The Iranians also brought in more senior diplomats and political figures, such as UN Ambassador Javad Zarif, to lead the Iranian delegation. The

---

[132]Seyyed Sajjad-Pour, "Iran and the Challenge of 11 September," *Global Dialogue* 4, no. 2 (2002): 7.

[133]Richardson.

69

Geneva Contact Group, now focused on Iraq, and with higher-level political appointees involved, gradually became less productive.[134] Few recognized that the best opportunity yet for rapprochement was slowly slipping away.

The Bush Doctrine

Throughout the remainder of 2002 and into early 2003, the administration's incoherent Iran policy seemed to conspire with world events to marginalize the State Department's Geneva dialogue, and empower neocon hubris on the issue of rapprochement with Iran. In July 2002, thousands of students and reformists marched on Tehran in commemoration of the July 1999 Reformist Revolution, and the influential Ayatollah Jalaleddin Taheri resigned after publicly criticizing regime hardliners for blocking Khatami's reforms. When several newspapers published Taheri's letter of resignation, Iran's judiciary conservatives shut down their offices and arrested reformist activists.[135] On July 12th, President Bush publicly denounced Iran's "uncompromising, destructive policies" and urged the Iranian government to "listen to their hopes," in what was meant as an expression of support for the reformist agenda.[136] The reformers, however, complained that Bush's comments only compromised their efforts. Iran Foreign Ministry spokesman Hamid Reza Asefi claimed Bush was using "bold and decayed tactics" to divide Iranians and their government.[137] Iranian Foreign Minister Kamal Kharrazi summarized the Iranian perspective best when he said:

---

[134]Parsi, *Treacherous Alliance*, 241; Pollack, 353; U.S. Congress.

[135]Pollack, 353-354.

[136]Pars Times, "Bush Urges Iran's Unelected Rulers to Listen to Voices of Their People," July 12, 2002, http://www.parstimes.com/news/archive/2002/washfile005.html (accessed February 2, 2013).

[137]Voice of America, "Iran Criticizes President Bush's Comments on Dissident Cleric," July 14, 2002, http://www.voanews.com/content/a-13-a-2002-07-14-6-iran-66500677/552934.html (accessed March 29, 2013).

That was another example of intervention in Iranian internal affairs. The current debates that exist between so-called reformists and conservatives is the nature of the system which allows people to express themselves. The reaction of the Americans toward this model was a mistake. The solution is a model based on the principles of Islam and democracy.[138]

Despite the increased rhetoric, many in Iran still supported a policy of reengagement. During the summer of 2002, the Majles commissioned a study to gauge public opinion on the issue of relations with America. The results revealed that 74 percent of Iranians over the age of 15 supported dialogue with the United States.[139] Many in the administration, however, ignored this sentiment.

Then on July 25th, the U.S. Senate adopted Resolution 306, labeling Iran "an ideological dictatorship presided over by an unelected Supreme Leader," and claiming "that President Muhammad Khatami's rhetoric has not been matched by his actions; whereas President Khatami clearly lacks the ability and inclination to change the behavior" of the government. As if these accusations were not damaging enough, the resolution went on to charge that, "Whereas since the terrorist attacks (of 9/11), and despite rhetorical protestations to the contrary, the Government of Iran has actively and repeatedly sought to undermine the United States war on terror." The Senate recommended that,

> Legitimizing the regime in Iran stifles the growth of the genuine democratic forces in Iran and does not serve the national security interests of the United States; positive gestures of the United States toward Iran should be directed toward the (people not the government); and it should be the policy of the United States to seek a genuine democratic government in Iran.[140]

[138]Slavin, "Q&A with Iranian Foreign Minister Kamal Kharrazi."

[139]BBC News World Edition, "Poll on US Ties Rocks Iran," October 2, 2002, http://news.bbc.co.uk/2/hi/middle_east/2294509.stm (accessed February 2, 2013).

[140]Pars Times, "Senate Resolution Says U.S. Should Seek Genuine Democracy in Iran," July 26, 2002, http://www.parstimes.com/news/archive/2002/washfile006.html (accessed February 2, 2013).

On August 2, 2002, in a speech before the Washington Institute for Near East Policy, Zalmay Khalilzad introduced the administration's new *Dual Track* foreign policy for Iran. Khalilzad explained that the United States would continue to oppose Iran's destructive and unacceptable behavior while laying out a positive vision for the Iranian people. The justification for this policy, he explained, was based on two fundamental principles: that the United States will confront threats before they manifest, and when given the choice, people will choose freedom. Khalilzad described the standard list of grievances regarding Iran: allegations that Iran was sheltering al Qaeda, support for international terrorism via Hizbollah, opposition to the existence of Israel, pursuit of nuclear weapons, and the unelected nature of Iran's government. He said, "U.S. policy is not to impose change on Iran but to support the Iranian people in their quest to decide their own destiny," yet the only strategy that Khalilzad offered to accomplish this change was his assurance that the United States would "continue to speak out in support of the Iranian people."[141]

This Dual Track policy was based on one of four pillars espoused in the soon to be released Bush Doctrine, the freedom agenda. President Bush's freedom agenda was the idealistic justification for the other three more controversial pillars of the Bush Doctrine: no distinction between terrorists and states that sponsor them, anticipatory self-defense, and preventive war. According to the administration's neocons, it was the responsibility of the United States, as the world's sole remaining superpower, to advance freedom and democracy throughout the world. This responsibility, they argued, was to not only advocate freedom and democracy as an

---

[141]Pars Times, "Senior U.S. Official Spells Out Dual-Track U.S. Policy Toward Iran," August 2, 2002, http://www.parstimes.com/news/archive/2002/washfile007.html (accessed February 2, 2013).

alternative to tyranny, but committed the United States to implementing these changes where possible, a sharp departure from the more realist foreign policies of the past 12 years.[142]

Then on August 14, 2002, the National Council of Resistance of Iran (the exiled political wing of the MeK) shocked the international community by revealing the existence of two previously undisclosed nuclear research facilities in Iran. According to the report, Iran had constructed a heavy-water production plant at Arak (for producing weapons grade plutonium) and a gas-centrifuge plant at Natanz (for producing highly enriched uranium). Iran was a signatory to the Nuclear Non-Proliferation Treaty (NNPT), but the International Atomic Energy Agency (IAEA) was unaware of the existence of either facility. The evidence was damning, and it appeared Iran's nuclear weapons program had progressed more rapidly than anyone estimated.[143] For the administration's neocons, this only confirmed their suspicion that Iran could not be trusted.

In late August, in preparation for the release of the new national security strategy, the Pentagon was putting the finishing touches on the two most controversial aspects of the new Bush Doctrine: unilateralism and preemption. Douglas Feith summarized the Pentagon's position in a memorandum, signed by Rumsfeld on August 24, 2002, entitled "Sovereignty and Anticipatory Self Defense." In the memorandum, the Pentagon argued that the United States should now take unilateral, preemptive military action in the face of "danger posed by weapons of mass

---

[142]George W. Bush, *Decision Points* (USA: Crown Publishers, 2010), 397.

[143]Michael Eisenstadt, "Iran's Nuclear Program: Gathering Dust or Gaining Steam?" *Washington Institute*, Policy Watch 707, February 3, 2003, http://www.washingtoninstitute.org/ policy-analysis/view/irans-nuclear-program-gathering-dust-or-gaining-steam (accessed February 2, 2013); GlobalSecurity.org, "Nuclear Weapons—2002 Developments in Iran." http://www.globalsecurity.org/wmd/world/iran/nuke2002.htm (accessed February 2, 2013).

destruction."[144] The Pentagon had just made its argument for invading Iraq, but the recently disclosed details about Iran's nuclear program led many in the Pentagon to argue this policy should apply to Iran as well.

The State Department finally confirmed the reports about Iran's nuclear program during a December 13th press conference, when spokesman Richard Boucher acknowledged, "We've reached the conclusion that Iran is actively working to develop nuclear weapons capability."[145] On December 16th, Foreign Minister Kharrazi denied the allegations, and two days later, President Khatami said, "Iran is working under the supervision of the IAEA, and Iran is a signatory to the NNPT and does not seek nuclear arms."[146] Regardless of who was right, the allegations only made U.S.-Iran relations more complicated, and marginalized those within the Bush administration arguing for engagement. [147]

The Bush Doctrine was formally published in the 2002 National Security Strategy of the United States. Founded on the concepts of anticipatory self-defense and preventive war, the

---

[144]Rumsfeld, 423; The Rumsfeld Papers: Footnote #21, "Sovereignty and Anticipatory Self-Defense," August 24, 2002, http://www.rumsfeld.com/endnotes/chapter-30/ (accessed March 28, 2013).

[145]Pars Times, "State Department Says Iran Seeking To Develop Nuclear Weapons," December 13, 2002, http://www.parstimes.com/news/archive/2002/washfile011.html (accessed February 2, 2013).

[146]GlobalSecurity.org, "Nuclear Weapons—2002 Developments in Iran."

[147]IAEA inspections of the Iranian facilities in February 2003 not only confirmed the allegations, but also revealed that Iran had been enriching uranium for some time with uranium samples provided by Pakistan and China. In late 2003, Iran agreed to fully disclose its nuclear research program, suspend enrichment of uranium, and sign an additional NNPT protocol allowing for additional oversight. When the IAEA issued its formal findings in November 2003, it acknowledged that Iran had operated a clandestine nuclear program for 18 years, but admitted there was no evidence indicating Iran had tried to build a nuclear weapon, as asserted by the United States; Eisenstadt; GlobalSecurity.org, "Nuclear Weapons – 2003 Developments in Iran." http://www.globalsecurity.org/wmd/world/iran/nuke2003.html (accessed February 2, 2013); Pollack, 363-365; Joby Warrick and Glenn Kessler, "Iran Had Secret Nuclear Program, U.N. Agency Says; 'No Evidence' of Arms Plans; Probe Continues," *Washington Post,* November 11, 2003.

doctrine's four pillars were: (1) make no distinction between terrorists and nations that harbor them; (2) take the fight to the enemy overseas before they can attack us at home; (3) confront threats before they fully materialize; (4) advance liberty and hope as an alternative to repression and fear.[148] The neocons had finally won the broader policy debate for the global war on terror strategy. Now they intended to implement that strategy across the Middle East. Word spread during the fall of 2002 that the neocons, full of hubris, were now looking beyond Iraq. According to a senior British official, the mantra was "everyone wants to go to Baghdad. Real men want to go to Tehran."[149]

Mission Accomplished

In early 2003, the Geneva Contact Group, now dominated by discussions on Iraq, served only to reassure the Americans that Iran would not oppose an invasion via its Iraq proxies, and reassure the Iranians that the American led coalition would remove Saddam from power and include the Shia majority in any new government. Although the ongoing dialogue was not a priority for the Bush administration, it still represented the best chance for Khatami and the reformists. In March 2003, the Geneva dialogue reached the highest levels yet within both governments, when both Ryan Crocker and Zalmay Khalilzad met with Iran's UN Ambassador, Mohammad Javad Zarif, in Geneva to discuss Iraq.[150]

The American invasion of Iraq in late March 2003, and the fall of Baghdad on April 9th had profound impacts in the United States and Iran. American power and prestige was at its highest level in the region in decades. For the Bush administration, the quick, decisive victory

---

[148]Bush, 396-397.

[149]The Daily Beast, "Policy: Beyond Baghdad," *Newsweek Magazine,* Periscope, August 18, 2002, http://www.thedailybeast.com/newsweek/2002/08/18/periscope.html (accessed February 6, 2013).

[150]Pollack, 353-354.

reinforced the notion of American exceptionalism and the neocon belief that application of the Bush Doctrine in the region could create a domino effect of democratization in the Middle East. The Iranians were shocked. The American military had defeated in days the same army the Iranians had only fought to a standstill in nine years. The effects of the successful invasion reverberated through the Iranian government, particularly amongst the conservative hardliners, some of whom now agreed in principle that Iran should consider rapprochement with the United States. In an interview given in February 2003 (but not published until April 12th), Rafsanjani (now chairman of the Expediency Council—a bastion of conservatism) offered that if the Majles presented a proposal to normalize relations with the United States, the council would seriously consider the proposal, and even suggested that a national referendum could be held on the issue.[151] In early May, the Majles responded to Rafsanjani's suggestion, and voted in favor of restoring relations with the United States. An Iranian diplomat even publicly stated, "We are ready to discuss re-establishing relations on the basis of mutual respect."[152]

On May 3, 2003, Zalmay Khalilzad and Ryan Crocker met again with Javad Zarif to discuss Iraq through the Geneva Contact Group. At the meeting, Khalilzad told Zarif the United States had intelligence about a pending terror attack in the Persian Gulf area, and demanded that Iran provide any information it may have through its al Qaeda detainees. Zarif, weary of cooperating with the Americans and receiving nothing but antagonistic rhetoric in return, offered a compromise. Iran would provide a list of its al Qaeda detainees only if the United States would provide a list of names of its MeK detainees in Iraq (The MeK, detained by the U.S. military inside Iraq, was still on the State Department's list of terrorist organizations). Both sides agreed

---

[151]Stephen C. Fairbanks, "Tehran Debates U.S. Relations," *Radio Free Europe/Radio Liberty*, May 2, 2003, http://www.parstimes.com/news/archive/2003/us_iran_relations.html (accessed February 2, 2013).

[152]Slavin, "Iran, U.S. Holding Talks in Geneva; Ties Debated in Both Countries," *USA Today*, May 12, 2003.

to meet again later that same month to provide their government's response, but that meeting never took place.[153]

In a May 12, 2003 *USA Today* column, Barbara Slavin revealed the existence of the Geneva Contact Group, which according to her sources, had the explicit approval of Iran's conservative clerics.[154] Both the State Department and Iran's Foreign Ministry immediately downplayed the report. State Department spokesman Philip Reeker said, "Diplomatic relations are not what's on the table in discussions with Iran. This is not somehow a new opening of diplomatic relations. This is an opportunity to deal with some practical issues."[155] Iran Foreign Ministry spokesman Hamid Reza Asefi said, "During these negotiations, the issue of bilateral relations was not on the agenda and no negotiations were held in that regard."[156] The administration's Dual Track policy was certainly contradictory; while diplomats meeting privately believed their work might lead to improved relations, both governments were publicly denying that rapprochement was possible.

In what was likely the final nail in the coffin for this round of U.S.-Iran engagement, on May 12th, the same day the Geneva dialogue was exposed, multiple truck bombs detonated at three western housing complexes in Riyadh, killing over 20 people, including eight American

---

[153]Nicholas D. Kristof, "Diplomacy At Its Worst," *New York Times*, April 29, 2007; Nicholas D. Kristof, "Iran's Proposal for a 'Grand Bargain'," On the Ground, entry posted April 28, 2007, http://kristof.blogs.nytimes.com/2007/04/28/irans-proposal-for-a-grand-bargain/?pagewanted=print (accessed February 3, 2013); Parsi, *Treacherous Alliance,* 250.

[154]Slavin, "Iran, U.S. Holding Talks in Geneva; Ties Debated in Both Countries." *USA Today*, May 12, 2003

[155]Pars Times, "U.S., Iran Discussing Afghanistan, Iraq, Other Issues of Mutual Interest," May 12, 2003, http://www.parstimes.com/news/archives/2003/reeker.html (accessed February 2, 2013).

[156]The Guardian, "Talks Thaw U.S.-Iran Relations," May 12, 2003, http://www.guardian.co.uk/world/2003/may/12/usa.iran (accessed February 2, 2013).

citizens.[157] President Khatami immediately condemned the attacks, stating that terrorism "by any person or party, and for whatever goal, is condemned." He also reassured Iranians and Americans that despite "important and big" differences with Washington, the recently disclosed Geneva dialogue would continue.[158] Citing evidence yet to be publicly confirmed, the administration soon revealed that the United States had intercepted communications between the Riyadh cell responsible for the attacks and al Qaeda operatives hiding in eastern Iran. The intelligence indicated that Saif al-Adel, a senior al Qaeda member thought to have fled into eastern Iran, might have directed the attack, yet U.S. officials could not definitely say if Adel was responsible, or if he was still hiding in Iran. In response, the administration cancelled the May 21st meeting in Geneva between Khalilzad and Zarif, and instead sent a message through the Swiss Embassy in Tehran communicating America's "concern that individuals associated with AQ have planned and directed the attack in Saudi Arabia from inside Iran."[159] The message also included a final demand that Iran turn over all al Qaeda subjects in custody or hiding inside the country.[160]

The entire affair quickly degenerated into public accusations and counteraccusations. It was clear that many of the administration's neocons realized this was a crisis to exploit. Some assumed Iran was complicit or had simply ignored Khalilzad's May 3rd request. On May 21st, Iranian officials admitted that Iran had several al Qaeda operatives in custody, but denied any

---

[157]Steven R. Weisman, "Aftereffects: The Attack; Bush Condemns Saudi Blasts; 7 Americans are Dead," *New York Times*, May 14, 2003, http://www.nytimes.com/2003/05/14/world/aftereffects-the-attack-bush-condemns-saudi-blasts-7-americans-are-dead.html (accessed February 2, 2013).

[158]Associated Press, "Iran's Leader Condemns Saudi Attacks," *Washington Post*, May 15, 2003.

[159]Douglas Jehl and Eric Schmitt, "U.S. Suggests al Qaeda Cell in Iran Directed Saudi Bombings," *New York Times*, May 21, 2003, http://www.nytimes.com/2003/05/21/international/middleeast/21IRAN.html (accessed February 2, 2013).

[160] Jehl and Schmitt; Douglas Jehl, "Iran Said to Hold Qaeda's No. 3, but to Resist Giving Him Up," *New York Times*, August 2, 2003; Steven R. Weisman, "U.S. Demands That Iran Turn Over Qaeda Agents and Join Saudi Inquiry." *New York Times*, May 26, 2003.

knowledge of a plot from inside Iran. In a Sunday, May 25th interview on ABC's *This Week*, Javad Zarif said Tehran was cooperating in attempts to control al Qaeda, but would not respond to the "language of pressure." He also confirmed that Iran had arrested members of al Qaeda, but was interrogating them and would eventually share information with other governments.[161] Secretary Rumsfeld responded by saying there was "no question there have been and are today senior al Qaeda leaders in Iran. And they're busy."[162] Iran then responded to the American demands with a counteroffer: Iran would surrender its al Qaeda detainees, but only if the United States would turn over its MeK detainees in Iraq.[163]

The administration convened an NSC meeting (it is still unclear what level of meeting it was) on May 27th to discuss the evolving strategy for Iran, but even before the meeting, press reports indicated there was a major divide within the administration on Iran policy: the realists, in favor of diplomatic pressure and dialogue, versus the neocons, opposed to dialogue and in favor of regime change. Anonymous administration officials acknowledged the intelligence suggesting an al Qaeda—Iran connection was inconclusive, and warned that some in the administration were pushing for a more aggressive Iran policy, including a military strike against the Natanz nuclear facility or active support of Iranian opposition groups, including the MeK.[164] Regardless, while the exact details of that NSC meeting are still unknown, it is interesting that none of the NSC Principals, nor President Bush, discussed the dialogue with Iran, or the decision to end that

---

[161] Weisman, "U.S. Demands That Iran Turn Over Qaeda Agents and Join Saudi Inquiry."

[162] Kelli Arena and Elise Labott, "Iran Admits Holding al Qaeda Operatives," *CNN.com* World Edition, May 25, 2003, http://www.cnn.com/2003/WORLD/meast/05/22/alqaeda.iran/ index.html (accessed February 2, 2013).

[163] Arena and Labott; Jehl, "Iran Said to Hold Qaeda's No. 3, but to Resist Giving Him Up."; Barbara Slavin, "Mutual Terror Accusations Halt U.S.-Iran Talks." *USA Today*, May 21, 2003, http://usatoday30.usatoday.com/news/world/2003-05-21-iran-usat_x.html (accessed February 2, 2013); Weisman, "U.S. Demands That Iran Turn Over Qaeda Agents and Join Saudi Inquiry."

[164] Weisman, "U.S. Demands That Iran Turn Over Qaeda Agents and Join Saudi Inquiry."

dialogue, in any substantive manner in any of their memoirs. Although the administration sent no

formal response to Iran regarding their counteroffer, the American position was clear soon after

when U.S. forces in Iraq signed a ceasefire agreement with the MeK. The neocons had finally

won the internal debate within the administration on Iran policy, and as a result, the Geneva

dialogue was dead. Once again, a Bush administration decided to ignore Iran.

The Grand Bargain: Missed Opportunity

In 2006 and 2007, information from former Bush administration officials, Washington

insiders, and Iranian diplomats revealed previously undisclosed details about the U.S.-Iran

dialogue between 2001 and 2003, and what many believed was Iran's proposal for a grand

bargain with the United States. Concurrent with the Geneva Contact Group dialogue, a second,

semi-official back channel was developed between several intermediaries, including Dr.

Hooshang Amirahmadi (founder and president of the American Iranian Council, a U.S. based

non-partisan think tank) and recently retired Career Ambassador Thomas Pickering. This track-

two diplomacy began back in August 2002, after Javad Zarif (James Dobbins' counterpart at the

Bonn Conference) was appointed as Iran's Ambassador to the UN.[165]

---

[165]BBC News, "Washington 'Snubbed Iran Offer,'" January 18, 2007, http://news.bbc.co.uk/go/pr/fr/-/2/hi/middle_east/6274147.stm (accessed January 29, 2013); Glenn Kessler, "2003 Memo Says Iranian Leaders Backed Talks," *Washington Post*, February 14, 2007, http://www.washingtonpost.com/wp-dyn/content/article/2007/02/13/AR2007021301363_pf.html (accessed February 3, 2013); Glenn Kessler, "In 2003, U.S. Spurned Iran's Offer of Dialogue," *Washington Post,* June 18, 2006, http://www.washingtonpost.com/wp-dyn/content/article/2006/06/17/AR2006061700727.html (accessed February 2, 2013); Kristof, "Diplomacy At Its Worst."; Parsi, *Treacherous Alliance*, 243-249; Trita Parsi, "Iran the Key in U.S. Change on Iraq," *Asia Times*, November 11, 2006, http://www.atimes.com/atimes/Middle_East/HK11Ak04.html (accessed February 3, 2013); Gareth Porter, "Burnt Offering," *The American Prospect* 17, iss. 6 (2006): 20-25; Gareth Porter, "How Neo-Cons Sabotaged Iran's Help on al Qaeda," *Global Information Network*, February 22, 2006; Gareth Porter,"Cheney-led 'Cabal' Blocked 2003 Nuclear Talks with Iran," *Global Information Network*, March 29, 2006; Slavin, "A Broken Engagement," 39-43.

In September 2002, Zarif hosted a dinner at his residence for several retired but still influential American ambassadors—Thomas Pickering, Frank Wisner, Nicholas Platt, William Miller and Richard Murphy, as well as Dr. Hooshang Amirahmadi. The group's discussion focused on how to improve U.S.-Iran relations based on cooperation over Afghanistan and Iraq. Zarif, who had worked so well with James Dobbins at the Bonn Conference, described the mood of distrust within the Iranian government, specifically the perception that despite Iran's positive gestures on Afghanistan, Bush's response was the axis of evil label and accusations that Iran was supporting al Qaeda. According to Zarif, Iran was confident the United States would invade Iraq, and several attendees expressed concern that Iran could be targeted next by the administration if relations did not significantly improve. Ambassador Pickering then posed a direct question to Zarif: was Iran interested in rapprochement? Zarif replied that Iran was not predisposed against normalizing relations. Ambassador Pickering then made the proposal, that for rapprochement to occur, both nations must express the political will to do so, agree on a roadmap to normalize diplomatic relations, and identify key issues to be resolved in the process. Zarif concurred, but countered that the Bush administration must first demonstrate its resolve to repair relations with Iran. The group agreed to continue working together to develop a broad plan for rapprochement (acknowledging the sensitive nature of this issue for both sides), while the Geneva dialogue would remain the official channel for discussions on Iraq and Afghanistan.[166]

Later that same month the group met again at Zarif's residence, but this time Iranian Foreign Minister Kamal Kharazi was in attendance, as well as two representatives from Senators Joseph Biden and Chuck Hagel. Kharazi dominated the discussion, expressing his disbelief at how the administration had responded to Iranian cooperation in Afghanistan over the past 11 months. When asked if Iran would be willing to normalize relations with the U.S., Kharazi

---

[166]Kristof, "Iran's Proposal for a 'Grand Bargain.'"

81

concurred, but included the caveat that the United States must signal a change in its rhetoric towards Iran. Throughout that evening and early into the next morning, the group developed a rough roadmap, identifying national aims and a process to normalize relations. Kharazi also committed to work with Zarif over the next several months to draft an official Iranian proposal.[167]

The next week, in early October 2002, Dr. Amirahmadi met with Khalilzad and Hillary Mann at the NSC, and informed them of the tentative agreement to develop a joint statement of principles to normalize relations. According to Dr. Amirahmadi, after a two-hour discussion Khalilzad admitted, "In principle, there is no problem with the proposal," but added that it must be approved by the administration. Over the next several weeks, Dr. Amirahmadi and Ambassador Pickering also met with Ryan Crocker and Assistant Secretary of State William Burns to discuss the tentative agreement with Iran's Foreign Ministry, but they never received a response from the administration.[168]

On the Iranian side, the proposal was taken much more seriously. Kharazi and Zarif brought in Kharazi's nephew, Sadegh Kharazi (Iran's Ambassador to France and son-in-law to Khamenei) to refine the terms of the proposal. Sadegh Kharazi worked closely with the Swiss Ambassador in Tehran, Tim Guldimann (who officially represented U.S. interests in Tehran and had been used previously by the Bush administration to pass sensitive messages to the Iranian government), to develop a proposal acceptable to leaders on both sides. According to Guldimann, the Iranian diplomats insisted on the utmost secrecy regarding this proposal. Throughout late April and into early May 2003, the proposal was refined and approved by Iran's foreign ministry, President Khatami, and Supreme Leader Khamenei. Khamenei insisted the proposal be approved in advance by the Bush administration through a discreet bilateral channel, for fear that if rejected

---

[167]Ibid.
[168]Ibid.

and exposed, it would undermine his support from the conservative hardliners opposed to any efforts at rapprochement. Guldimann decided to use someone he trusted, Ohio Congressman Bob Ney, a proponent of the U.S.-Iran dialogue, as an intermediary.[169]

Although slightly separate versions of this grand bargain proposal exist, they are all fundamentally the same in that each document identified goals for both nations, as well as a roadmap for normalizing relations. In return for the United States formally recognizing the Islamic Republic as the legitimate government of Iran, abolishing all sanctions, allowing Iran access to peaceful nuclear technology, and membership in the World Trade Organization, Iran agreed to fully comply with IAEA transparency requirements, sign the secondary protocol to the NNPT, take decisive action against al Qaeda in Iran, cease all support to HAMAS, pressure Hizbollah to transform into an exclusively political organization, and pledged to support a two-state solution in Palestine. Everything was finally on the table.[170]

In late April, Guldimann sent a draft of the Iranian proposal to Hillary Mann, now at the State Department, in what was likely a final effort to feel out the administration. Mann forwarded her summary memorandum with the proposal to her boss, Richard Haas, who sent it to Powell.[171] In early May 2003, Guldimann flew to Washington, D.C. and hand delivered Iran's official proposal (with an eleven-page summary of his conversations with the Iranians) to Congressman Ney. According to Trita Parsi, Ney acknowledged, "this is it…this is the one that will make it happen." [172] Ney immediately sent the proposal to his longtime friend and presidential advisor Karl Rove, who promptly called Ney to confirm the document's authenticity, and agreed to present the proposal to the president. Several days later, on May 4th, Guldimann faxed a

---

[169]Ibid.; Parsi, *Treacherous Alliance,* 243-249.

[170]Kristof, "Iran's Proposal for a 'Grand Bargain.'"

[171]Richardson.

[172]Parsi, *Treacherous Alliance,* 247.

summary of the Iranian proposal with a cover letter (authenticating the documents authenticity and approval by Khamenei, Khatami, and Kharazi) to the State Department and the U.S. Ambassador in Geneva.[173]

There was no response. The only official response from the administration came in the form of a warning to the Swiss government that their ambassador had overstepped his mandate.[174] According to Hillary Mann, Powell later told her, "It was a good memo. I couldn't sell it at the White House."[175] In response to questions about the proposal, Powell acknowledged, "We talked to the Iranians quietly up until 2003. The president chose not to continue that channel."[176] It is still unclear when or how the administration made the decision to ignore Iran's offer. According to Flynt Leverett, the administration failed to set up an interagency or NSC meeting to even discuss the proposal.[177] Leverett recalled, "the State Department knew it had no chance at the interagency level of arguing the case for it successfully...they weren't going to waste Powell's rapidly diminishing capital on something that unlikely."[178] According to Lawrence Wilkerson, former chief of staff to Secretary Powell, it was Rumsfeld and Cheney who were instrumental in dismissing the Iranian proposal, because Rumsfeld wanted to use the MeK to foment a popular uprising in Iran.[179] The State Department supported the proposal, but the neocons in the OSD and NSC won the debate. Wilkerson said, "We thought it was a very propitious moment to [make that proposal], but as soon as it got to the White House, and as soon as it got to the vice president's

---

[173]Kristof, "Iran's Proposal for a 'Grand Bargain.'"; Parsi, *Treacherous Alliance,* 247.

[174]Parsi, *Treacherous Alliance,* 249.

[175]Richardson.

[176]Ibid.

[177]Ibid.

[178]Porter, "Burnt Offering," 20-25.

[179]Parsi, "Iran the Key in U.S. Change on Iraq."

office, the old mantra of 'we don't talk to evil'...reasserted itself."[180] No one at the State

Department knew who or how the decision was made. Wilkerson later observed, "As with many

of these issues of national security decision-making, there are no fingerprints..." In the end,

according to Wilkerson, a "secret cabal" of neocons, led by Cheney and Rumsfeld, "got what it

wanted: no negotiations with Tehran."[181]

Despite the rhetoric, and the ambiguous Dual Track diplomacy, the administration had

not yet adopted an official Iran policy. Key decision makers were still too preoccupied with

Afghanistan and Iraq, and despite the insistence by some in the State Department that this

opportunity presented a strategic opening for U.S.-Iran dialogue, the neocons refused to allow it,

in the hopes of effecting regime change in the future. Although a draft National Security Policy

Directive (NSPD) on Iran had been in the process of interagency coordination within the NSC

since early 2002, it was undermined by officials in the vice president's office, and at the OSD,

where Douglas Feith preferred a policy of regime change.[182] The May 12th Riyadh attacks only

served to strengthen the neoconservative argument that Iran was sheltering al Qaeda and

undermining U.S. efforts in the war on terror. Apparently, by the May 27th NSC meeting,

Rumsfeld and Cheney had already convinced Bush to close the Geneva dialogue, and just as

previous presidents before him, Bush chose to isolate Iran.[183] As Trita Parsi observed, "it was

1991 all over again: there was no appreciation for Iran's strategic interest in a stable Middle East

and the possibility that Tehran wanted to patch up relations with the United States."[184] In the

shadow of 9/11, the neocons exploited threats of terrorism and the bipolar nature of Iran's

---

[180]BBC News, "Washington 'Snubbed Iran Offer.'"

[181]Porter, "Cheney-led 'Cabal' Blocked 2003 Nuclear Talks with Iran."

[182]Porter, "Cheney-led 'Cabal' Blocked 2003 Nuclear Talks with Iran."

[183]Porter, "Burnt Offering," 20-25.

[184]Parsi, *Treacherous Alliance*, 230.

political system to prevent a strategic rapprochement between both nations. The administration's policy position ultimately was—why talk when you can demand?

Days later, Feith and the neocons in the OSD released an alternative Iran NSPD. On May 30th, ABC News reported that the Pentagon had developed a plan which called for destabilizing the Iranian government "using all available points of pressure on the Iranian regime, including backing armed Iranian dissidents and employing the services of the Mujahideen e Kalq…"[185] The president's hubris towards Iran finally reached a pinnacle during the summer of 2003, when Jay Garner, the U.S. Administrator for Iraq, was asked by President Bush, "Hey, Jay, you want to do Iran?"[186] But the result of the administration's Iran policy was disastrous. Within months, Iranian proxies inside Iraq began training and arming Shia resistance groups, and by 2004, Iraq was embroiled in sectarian conflict and a growing insurgency.

The administration's rejection of Iran's grand bargain signaled the defeat of Khatami's reform movement, and solidified hardline conservative control over Iran's government. During the 2004 Majles elections, thousands of reformist candidates were banned from running, and the reformist movement suffered from a backlash as conservatives regained majority control. At the end of Khatami's second term in 2005, hardline conservative Mahmoud Ahmadinejad decisively defeated Rafsanjani in a presidential run-off election. After undermining the reformists and

---

[185]In fact, Larry Franklin, Feith's operative in OSD's Office of Special Plans (who had met with Ghobanifar in Rome in December 2001), provided a copy of the draft NSPD to an Israeli diplomat and two AIPAC lobbyists as early as February 2003 in an effort to pressure the administration to take a harder line with Iran. After a lengthy FBI espionage investigation, Franklin was sentenced to 12 years in prison on January 20, 2006 for passing classified information; Vince Cannistraro, "The Covert Iran Plan," *ABC News*, May 29, 2003, http://abcnews.go.com/US/story?id=90585&page=1#.UVcuh7-Viu1 (accessed March 29, 2013); David Johnston, "Pentagon Analyst Gets 12 Years for Disclosing Data," *New York Times*, January 20, 2006; Eric Lichtblau, "Pentagon Analyst Admits Sharing Secret Data," *New York Times*, October 6, 2005; Porter, "Cheney-led 'Cabal' Blocked 2003 Nuclear Talks with Iran."

[186]Bob Woodward, *State of Denial: Bush At War Part III* (London: Simon and Schuster, 2006), 224.

refusing to engage Iran while at the height of American power and prestige in the Middle East,

the administration finally came back to the table in 2005 and 2006 (using some of the same offers

the Clinton administration made in the late 1990s), however this time they were dealing with

Iran's own neoconservatives, who no longer believed they needed to negotiate with the United

States.[187]

Some still refuse to acknowledge this lost opportunity. Most of the Bush administration's

key decision makers remain silent about the Geneva dialogue and Iran's grand bargain proposal.

Others claim it was not legitimate, or that if the Iranians were serious about substantive

negotiations, it would have come through the Geneva Contact Group, and actions would have

matched rhetoric. John Bolton, commenting on the proposal that was faxed to the State

Department, said, "I've seen a variety of things; I'd rather not comment on exactly what they

were. I was aware of the proposal; I spoke to Secretary Powell about it. I thought it was a bad

idea and I told him so…I thought it was a fantasy." When asked if he thought it was legitimate,

Bolton said,

> I think all kinds of things come out of the Iranian regime that are intended to get gullible
> Americans to say that sweetness and light are about to break out, the consequence of
> which is to give Iran more time to do what it's busily been doing in an clandestine
> fashion for close to 20 years.[188]

Michael Rubin also argued in a 2007 article in the *Weekly Standard* that the Guldimann

memorandum was a fraud. But Rubin's credibility and perspective on this issue is suspect. From

[187]Hunter, *Iran's Foreign Policy in the Post-Soviet Era*, 63; Slavin, "A Broken Engagement," 39-43.

[188]PBS Frontline, "The "Grand Bargain" Fax: A Missed Opportunity?" http://www.pbs.org/wgbh/pages/frontline/showdown/themes/grandbargain.html (accessed January 29, 2013).

2002 to 2004, Rubin served as the Iraq-Iran International Security Affairs Advisor in the OSD,

right in the heart of the neoconservative cabal, as Wilkerson labeled it.[189]

Many are still convinced the United States lost what was the greatest opportunity yet for

rapprochement. Flynt Leverett later said,

> I thought it was an extraordinary proposal, basically on comparable scale to the kinds of representations from Zhou Enlai that were passed through Pakistan in 1971 that paved the way for Kissinger's secret trip to Beijing and then the Nixon trip to China. I thought they were proposing something on that scale of historic and strategic importance.

When asked if the United States should have made a deal, he said,

> From an American perspective it was absolutely the time to try and make a deal. We were at the height of our apparent power in the region. Iran was not yet spinning centrifuges, not yet enriching uranium. The president of Iran was not Mahmoud Ahmadinejad, but Mohammad Khatami. Iraq had not yet fallen apart. And early cooperation, I think, might have been very helpful in forestalling the worst of what we've seen in Iraq over the past four years.

Asked why the administration refused the deal, Leverett said, "Because important power centers

in the administration—the vice president, the secretary of defense, and I think in the end the

president himself—were opposed to this kind of diplomatic effort with Iran."[190]

> Richard Armitage, when asked if he was open to the idea of dialogue, said,

> We were open to it. As you know, we've argued that we need to speak with our enemies perhaps even more than we need to speak to our friends. So we took the point of view that no matter how difficult relations are with any one country, we should not cut ourselves off from them, and we ought to talk to them. So I'll say…Secretary Powell and I, were very interested.

When asked about Cheney and Rumsfeld's positions, he said,

> I suspect they were much less interested, it appears. And the fact that its been so difficult even now, two years-plus on, to get real engagement with the Iranians, notwithstanding the significant efforts, as I understand them, of the secretary of state, shows that some people in the administration are still disinclined to engage.[191]

---

[189]Michael Rubin, "The Guldimann Memorandum," *The Weekly Standard*, 13, iss. 6, (October 22, 2007): 14-15.

[190]PBS Frontline. "The "Grand Bargain" Fax: A Missed Opportunity?"

[191]Ibid.

Mohammad Ali Abtahi, Iran's vice president in 2003, when asked if the proposal was

approved by the Iranian government, said, "What is certain is that it didn't get anywhere and that

case is now closed."[192] Middle East and Iran expert Vali Nasr, when asked why the Iranians did

not use the Geneva channel to pass this message, said,

> There are many reasons why it came through the channels that it did, because it was a
> very bold offer on the part of those who put it forward…it was a huge risk. And there is
> reason why they would not want to stick their neck out [without] having a certain degree
> of assurance that it would be reciprocated. So the Khatami government, the reformist
> government, is making one last effort to make a pitch to the U.S., it is running a risk. And
> I assume that their hope was that the U.S. would test the proposal by coming back…and
> the test came back negative.[193]

CONCLUSION

The Ayatollah Khamenei once said about America, "Iran's problem was that it had an

enemy who was always after a new excuse."[194] One could also argue the opposite is true. Both

sides are at fault for perpetuating the mutual distrust of the past three decades. America's failure

to recognize the significance of 1953, and subsequent policy decisions in support of the shah,

only reinforced the view that America was the primary source of Persian humiliation. Iran's

emotional response in 1979 not only humiliated the United States, but also created what appeared

to be an insurmountable sociopolitical divide between both nations. Despite the rhetoric, the

reality of the international system forced Iran's revolutionary idealists to act like pragmatists, and

this afforded both sides with opportunities to reengage. Although unsuccessful, each failure

provided lessons for future generations to apply. Foremost, nations cannot engage in an effective

dialogue without formal diplomatic relations. Backchannels and intermediaries engender

misunderstanding and distrust. Next, the United States must have a clear Iran policy, and an

effectively resourced strategy to implement that policy. This strategy must take into account the

---

[192]Ibid.

[193]Ibid.

[194]Hunter, *Iran's Foreign Policy in the Post-Soviet Era*, 61.

fragmented nature of Iran's political system. Although some perceive it to be bipolar, or even duplicitous, the United States must patiently engage Iran. As history has shown, once Iran reemerges as part of the international community of nations, its political system will mature. Finally, rapprochement must be a priority; America can no longer afford to ignore Iran. Rapprochement must be the policy end goal for both Iran and the United States. Both President Clinton and President Khatami laid the groundwork for rapprochement through their track-two and dialogue of civilizations foreign policies, but as they both realized, this process needed more time and common ground to proceed.

The events of 9/11 created an unprecedented opportunity for a strategic rapprochement between the United States and the Islamic Republic of Iran. Cooperation against al Qaeda and the Taliban in Afghanistan led to the bilateral dialogue of the Geneva Contact Group, where the Bush administration accomplished what no other president since 1979 thought possible: direct negotiations with Iran on issues of mutual interest. Even when that bilateral channel became less productive, Iran continued a process of dialogue and negotiation, culminating with the grand bargain proposal in May 2003. Common ground existed, but the Bush administration was too impatient.

In hindsight, it is now clear why the Bush administration adopted a policy of confrontation and demand over dialogue with Iran. The Taliban were defeated, Iraq was liberated, other rogue states like Libya were beginning to come around, and for the first time in over 20 years, Iran was willing to talk with the United States. American power and prestige was at its height, and the implications of 9/11 justified a more aggressive, preemptive foreign policy. The Bush neoconservatives, dominating the NSC policy formulation process, viewed Iran through the same lens they viewed al Qaeda, the Taliban, and Saddam Hussein. Americans have a short attention span: the administration responded to Iran through the context of 1979, yet few considered that most Iranians still viewed America through the events of 1953. Regime change

90

was the wrong policy for Iran. The militarized foreign policy approach that the administration thought worked so well in Afghanistan and Iraq was not relevant to Iran. As the Bush administration was about to discover, one cannot apply a singular policy to the complexity of the Middle East. The Bush Doctrine did just that. If realist foreign policy is disciplined, judging situations on a case-by-case basis and through a pragmatic lens, then the Bush Doctrine was lazy foreign policy.[195] President Bush missed what was likely the greatest opportunity yet for a strategic rapprochement with the Islamic Republic.

George W. Bush failed to apply the lessons of his predecessors' experiences dealing with Iran, particularly his father's decision to ignore Iran in 1992. Ten years later, the implications of the Bush administration's decision to end the Geneva dialogue and ignore Iran's grand bargain proposal continues to haunt the Obama administration, and the threat of a rogue, isolated, and nuclear-armed Iran is now a distinct possibility. One can only hope, as Madeline Albright and Mohammad Khatami suggested, that pragmatists on both sides will adjust their lens, put aside differences, and find common ground.

James Dobbins, testifying before Congress, put it best when he suggested,

It is time to apply to Iran the policies which won the Cold War, liberated the Warsaw Pact, and reunited Europe: détente and containment, communication whenever possible, and confrontation whenever necessary. We spoke to Stalin's Russia. We spoke to Mao's China. In both cases, greater mutual exposure changed their system, not ours. It's time to speak to Iran, unconditionally, and comprehensively.[196]

---

[195]Bartholomew H. Sparrow, "Realism's Practitioner: Brent Scowcroft and the Making of the New World Order, 1989-1993," *Diplomatic History* 34, no. 1 (January 2010): 166, 170-171.

[196]Dobbins, "Negotiating with Iran."

BIBLIOGRAPHY

Afghanistan Government. "Afghan Bonn Agreement: Agreement on Provisional Arrangements in Afghanistan Pending the Re-establishment of Permanent Government Institutions." http://www.afghangovernment.com/AfghanAgreementBonn.html (accessed July 26, 2012).

Afrasiabi, Kaveh, and Abbas Maleki. "Iran's Foreign Policy after 11 September." *Brown Journal Of World Affairs* 9, no. ii (2003): 255-265.

Ansari, Ali M. *Confronting Iran: The Failure of American Foreign Policy and the Next Great Crisis in the Middle East.* New York: Basic Books, 2006.

Arena, Kelli and Elise Labott. "Iran Admits Holding al Qaeda Operatives." *CNN.com World Edition* (May 25, 2003). http://www.cnn.com/2003/WORLD/meast/05/22/alqaeda.iran/index.html (accessed February 2, 2013).

Associated Press. "Iran's Leader Condemns Saudi Attacks." *Washington Post*, May 15, 2003.

Barsamian, David, Noam Chomsky, Ervand Abrahamian, and Nahid Mozaffari. *Targeting Iran.* San Francisco: City Lights Books, 2007.

Bartleby.com. "Inaugural Address of President George H. W. Bush, Friday, January 20, 1989." http://www.bartleby.com/124/pres63.html (accessed March 15, 2013).

BBC News. "Washington 'Snubbed Iran Offer.'" January 18, 2007. http://news.bbc.co.uk/go/pr/fr/-/2/hi/middle_east/6274147.stm (accessed January 29, 2013).

BBC News, Middle East Online Edition. "Iranian Commanders Assassinated." October 18, 2009. http://news.bbc.co.uk/2/hi/middle_east/8312964.stm (accessed January 31, 2013).

BBC News World Edition. "Poll on US Ties Rocks Iran." 2 October 2002. http://news.bbc.co.uk/2/hi/middle_east/2294509.stm (accessed February 2, 2013).

Berman, Ilan. *Tehran Rising: Iran's Challenge to the United States.* Lanham, MD: National Book Network, 2005.

Bill, James A. *The Eagle and the Lion: The Tragedy of American-Iranian Relations.* New Haven, CT: Yale University Press, 1988.

Bush, George W. *Decision Points.* USA: Crown Publishers, 2010.

Cannistraro, Vince. "The Covert Iran Plan." *ABC News*, May 29, 2003. http://abcnews.go.com/US/story?id=90585&page=1#.UVcuh7-Viu1 (accessed March 29, 2013).

Carter, Stephen. "Iran's Interest in Afghanistan and their Implications for NATO." *International Journal* (Autumn 2010): 982.

CBS News. "Iran Gave U.S. Help On Al Qaeda After 9/11." September 4, 2009. http://www.cbsnews.com/2102-202_162-4508360.html?tag=contentMain;contentBody (accessed March 12, 2013).

CNN.com. "Transcript of Interview with Iranian President Mohammad Khatami." January 7, 1998. http://www.cnn.com/WORLD/9801/07/iran/interview.html (accessed February 5, 2013).

CNN.com World Edition. "Attacks Draw Mixed Response in Mideast." September 12, 2001.
    http://www.archives.cnn.com/2001/WORLD/europe/09/12/mideast.reaction/index.htm
    (accessed March 10, 2013).

Cumings, Bruce, Ervand Abrahamian, and Modhe Ma'oz. *Inventing the Axis of Evil: The Truth
    about North Korea, Iran, and Syria*. New York: New Press, 2004.

The Daily Beast. "Policy: Beyond Baghdad." *Newsweek Magazine,* Periscope, August 18, 2002.
    http://www.thedailybeast.com/newsweek/2002/08/18/periscope.html (accessed February
    6, 2013).

Daniel, Elton. *The History of Iran*. Westport, CT: Greenwood Press, 2001.

Daniszewski, John. "Iran's Own Desert Storm." *Los Angeles Times*, March 21, 2000.

Dobbins, James. "Negotiating with Iran: Reflections from Personal Experience." *Washington
    Quarterly* (January 2010): 149-154.

_____. "Negotiating with Iran." Testimony presented before the House Committee on
    Oversight and Government Reform, Subcommittee on National Security and Foreign
    Affairs on November 7, 2007. http://www.rand.org/pubs/ testimonies/CT293.html
    (accessed March 1, 2013).

Eisenstadt, Michael. "Iran's Nuclear Program: Gathering Dust or Gaining Steam?" *The
    Washington Institute, Policy Watch* 707 (February 3, 2003).
    http://www.washingtoninstitute.org/policy-analysis/view/irans-nuclear-program-
    gathering-dust-or-gaining-steam (accessed February 2, 2013).

Fairbanks, Stephen C. "Tehran Debates U.S. Relations." *Radio Free Europe/Radio Liberty* (May
    2, 2003). http://www.parstimes.com/news/archive/2003/us_iran_relations.html (accessed
    February 2, 2013).

Fathi, Nazila. "A Nation Challenged: Tehran; Iran Softens Tone Against the United States." *New
    York Times*, September 21, 2001. http://www.newyorktimes.com/2001/ 09/21/world/a-
    nation-challenged-tehran-iran-softens-tone-against-the-united-states.html (accessed
    March 28, 2013).

Federation of American Scientists. "Secretary of State Madeleine K. Albright Remarks at 1998
    Asia Society Dinner." June 17, 1998. http://www.fas.org/news/iran/1998/980617a.html
    (accessed March 28, 2013).

Federation of American Scientists. "Secretary of State Madeleine K. Albright Remarks before the
    American-Iranian Council." March 17, 2000.
    http://www.fas.org/news/iran/2000/0003317.html (accessed March 28, 2013).

Federation of American Scientists-Intelligence Resource Program. "Bush Administration
    National Security Directive 26: U.S. Policy Toward the Persian Gulf."
    http://www.fas.org/irp/offdocs/nsd/nsd26.pdf (accessed March 15, 2013).

Feith, Douglas J. *War and Decision: Inside the Pentagon at the Dawn of the War on Terrorism*.
    New York: Harper Collins, 2009.

Frum, David. *The Right Man: An Inside Account of the Bush White House*. Westminster, MD:
    Random House, 2003.

Gardiner, Sam. "Dangerous and Getting More Dangerous: The Delicate Situation Between the
    United States and Iran." A Century Foundation Report, 2008.

Gasiorowski, Mark J. "The Power Struggle in Iran." *Middle East Policy* 7, no. 4 (October 2000): 22-36.

GlobalSecurity.org. "Weapons of Mass Destruction: Bushehr Background." http://www.globalsecurity.org/wmd/world/iran/bushehr-intro.htm (accessed March 10, 2013).

_____. "Nuclear Weapons—2002 Developments in Iran." http://www.globalsecurity.org/wmd/world/iran/nuke2002.htm (accessed February 2, 2013).

Gordon, Michael R., and Bernard E. Trainor. *Cobra II: The Inside Story of the Invasion and Occupation of Iraq*. New York: Pantheon Books, 2006.

The Guardian. "Talks Thaw U.S.-Iran Relations." May 12, 2003. http://www.guardian.co.uk/world/2003/may/12/usa.iran (accessed February 2, 2013).

Hardy, Roger. "Bush 'endorses' Palestinian state." *BBC News*, Middle East Online Edition, October 2, 2001. http://news.bbc.co.uk/2/hi/middle_east/1575090.stm (accessed January 30, 2013).

Hersh, Seymour M. "The Iran Game." *The New Yorker* 77, no. 38 (December 3, 2011): 42.

Hertzberg, Hendrick. "Axis Praxis." *The New Yorker* (January 13, 2003). http://www.newyorker.com/archive/2003/01/13/030113ta_talk_hertzberg?printable=true (accessed January 29, 2013).

Hunter, Shireen T. *Iran's Foreign Policy in the Post-Soviet Era: Resisting the New International Order*. Santa Barbara: Praeger, 2010.

_____. *Iran After Khomeini*. The Washington Papers, vol. 156. New York: Praeger, 1992.

Israel Ministry of Foreign Affairs. "Seizing of the Palestinian Weapons Ship Karine A." January 4, 2002. http://www.mfa.gov.il/MFA/Government/Communiques/2002/Seizing%20of%20the%20Palestinian%20weapons%20ship%20Karine%20A%20-.html (accessed July 26, 2012).

_____. "Statement by IDF Chief-of-Staff Lt.-Gen. Shaul Mofaz regarding interception of ship Karine A." (January 4, 2002). http:www.mfa.gov.il/MFA/Government/Speeches+by+Israeli+leaders/2002/Statement+by+IDF+Chief-of-Staff+Lt-Gen+Shaul+Mofaz.html (accessed July 26, 2012).

Jehl, Douglas. "Iran Said to Hold Qaeda's No. 3, but to Resist Giving Him Up." *New York Times*, August 2, 2003.

Jehl, Douglas, and Eric Schmitt. "U.S. Suggests al Qaeda Cell in Iran Directed Saudi Bombings." *New York Times*, May 21, 2003. http://www.nytimes.com/2003/05/21/international/middleeast/21IRAN.html (accessed 2 February2013).

Johnston, David. "Pentagon Analyst Gets 12 Years for Disclosing Data." *New York Times*, January 20, 2006.

Katzman, Kenneth. "Congressional Research Service Report for Congress: The Iran-Libya Sanctions Act (ILSA)." http://www.dtic.mil/cgi-bin/GetTRDoc?AD=ADA475663 (accessed January 21, 2013).

Keddie, Nickie R. *Modern Iran: Roots and Results of Revolution*. New Haven, CT: Yale University Press, 2003.

Kelley, Matt. "Iran Has Allowed Taliban, al-Qaida Members to Escape, Rumsfeld Says." *Associated Press*, February 3, 2002. http://www2.ljworld.com/news/2002/feb/03/ iran_has_allowed/ (accessed January 30, 2013).

Kessler, Glenn. "2003 Memo Says Iranian Leaders Backed Talks." *Washington Post*, February 14, 2007. http://www.washingtonpost.com/wp-dyn/content/article/2007/02/13/ AR2007021301363_pf.html (accessed February 3, 2013).

_____. "In 2003, U.S. Spurned Iran's Offer of Dialogue." *Washington Post,* June 18, 2006. http://www.washingtonpost.com/wp-dyn/content/article/2006/06/17/ AR2006061700727.html (accessed February 2, 2013).

Kristof, Nicholas D. "Diplomacy At Its Worst." *New York Times*, April 29, 2007.

_____. "Iran's Proposal for a 'Grand Bargain'." On the Ground, entry posted April 28, 2007, http://kristof.blogs.nytimes.com/2007/04/28/irans-proposal-for-a-grand- bargain/?pagewanted=print (accessed February 3, 2013).

Ledeen, Michael Arthur. *Accomplice to Evil: Iran and the War Against the West.* New York: Truman Talley Books/St. Martin's Press, 2009.

Leverett, Flynt. "Illusion and Reality." *The American Prospect* (September 2006). http://newamerica.net/publications/articles/2006/illusion_and_reality (accessed March 10, 2013).

Leverett, Flynt, and Hillary Mann Leverett. "Letters to the Editor: Who's Misreading Tehran?" *Foreign Policy*, 181 (September/October 2010): 14-15.

Lichtblau, Eric. "Pentagon Analyst Admits Sharing Secret Data." *New York Times*, October 6, 2005.

Marshall, Joshua Micah, Laura Rozen, and Paul Glastris. "Iran-Contra II?" *Washington Monthly*, October 2004.

Mufson, Steven, and Marc Kaufman. "Longtime Foes U.S., Iran Explore Improved Relations." *The Washington Post*, October 29, 2001.

Parsi, Trita. *Treacherous Alliance: The Secret Dealings of Israel, Iran, and the U.S.* New Haven, CT: Yale University Press, 2007.

_____. "Iran the Key in U.S. Change on Iraq." *Asia Times*, November 11, 2006. http://www.atimes.com/atimes/Middle_East/HK11Ak04.html (accessed February 3, 2013).

Pars Times. "Algiers Accords, January 19, 1981." www.parstimes.com/history/ algiers_accords.pdf (accessed March 1, 2013).

_____. "Bush Urges Iran's Unelected Rulers to Listen to Voices of Their People," July 12, 2002. http://www.parstimes.com/news/archive/2002/washfile005.html (accessed February 2, 2013).

_____. "Senate Resolution Says U.S. Should Seek Genuine Democracy in Iran." July 26, 2002. http://www.parstimes.com/news/archive/2002/washfile006.html (accessed February 2, 2013).

_____. "Senior U.S. Official Spells Out Dual-Track U.S. Policy Toward Iran." August 2, 2002. http://www.parstimes.com/news/archive/2002/washfile007.html (accessed February 2, 2013).

_____. "State Department Says Iran Seeking To Develop Nuclear Weapons." December 13, 2002. http://www.parstimes.com/news/archive/2002/washfile011.html (accessed February 2, 2013).

_____. "U.S., Iran Discussing Afghanistan, Iraq, Other Issues of Mutual Interest." May 12, 2003. http://www.parstimes.com/news/archives/2003/reeker.html (accessed February 2, 2013).

PBS Frontline. "Target America." http://www.pbs.org/wgbh/pages/frontline/shows/target/etc/cron.html (accessed March 10, 2013).

_____. "Terror and Tehran: Does America's war on terror hold democracy hostage in Iran?" http://www.pbs.org/wgbh/pages/frontline/shows/tehran/ (accessed March 1, 2013).

_____. "The 'Grand Bargain' Fax: A Missed Opportunity?" http://www.pbs.org/wgbh/pages/frontline/showdown/themes/grandbargain.html (accessed January 29, 2013).

_____. "Terror and Tehran: Does America's war on terror hold democracy hostage in Iran?" http://www.pbs.org/wgbh/pages/frontline/shows/tehran/ (accessed March 1, 2013).

Pollack, Kenneth M. *The Persian Puzzle: The Conflict Between Iran and America.* New York: Random House, 2004.

Porter, Gareth. "Burnt Offering." *The American Prospect* 17, no. 6 (2006): 20-25.

_____. "How Neo-Cons Sabotaged Iran's Help on al Qaeda." *Global Information Network*, February 22, 2006.

_____. "Cheney-led 'Cabal' Blocked 2003 Nuclear Talks with Iran." *Global Information Network*, March 29, 2006

Project for the New American Century. "Open Letter to President George W. Bush." September 20, 2001. http://www.newamericancentury.org/RebuildingAmericasDefenses.pdf (accessed February 6, 2013).

Rees, Matt, Massimo Calabresi, Jamil Hamad and Aharon Klein. "Postmarked Tehran." *Time*, 159 (January 21, 2002): 54.

Richardson, John H. "The Secret History of the Impending War with Iran That the White House Doesn't Want You to Know." *Esquire Magazine* (October 18, 2007). http://www.esquire.com/features/iranbriefing1107 (accessed March 1, 2013).

Risen, James. "Congress OKs House Plan to Fund Covert Action in Iran." *Los Angeles Times*, December 22, 1995. http://articles.latimes.com/1995-12-22/news/mn-16920_1_intelligence-budget (accessed March 1, 2013).

Rubin, Michael. "The Guldimann Memorandum." *The Weekly Standard* 13, no. 6 (October 22, 2007): 14-15.

Rumsfeld, Donald. *Known and Unknown: A Memoir.* New York: Penguin Group, 2011.

The Rumsfeld Papers. "Sovereignty and Anticipatory Self-Defense." (August 24, 2002). http://www.rumsfeld.com/endnotes/chapter-30/ (accessed March 28, 2013).

Sadat, Mir H., and James P. Hughes. "U.S.-Iran Engagement Through Afghanistan." *Middle East Policy* 17, no. 1 (2010): 3

Sajjad-Pour, Seyyed. "Iran and the Challenge of 11 September." *Global Dialogue* 4, no. 2 (2002): 7.

Sciolino, Elaine. "Iran Finds a Not-So-Great Satan on Its Doorstep." *New York Times*, September 20, 1998.

Sipress, Alan. "Bush's Speech Shuts Door on Tenuous Opening to Iran." *Washington Post*, February 4, 2002.

Sipress, Alan, and Steven Mufson. "U.S. Explores Recruiting Iran Into New Coalition." *Washington Post*, September 25, 2001.

Slavin, Barbara. "A Broken Engagement." *The National Interest*, no. 92 (November/December 2007): 39.

_____. *Bitter Friends, Bosom Enemies: Iran, the U.S., and the Twisted Path to Confrontation.* New York: St. Martin's Press, 2007.

_____. "Iran Seeks Help in Finding al-Qaeda, Taliban Fugitives." *USA Today*, February 6, 2002.

_____. "Iran, U.S. Holding Talks in Geneva; Ties Debated in Both Countries." *USA Today*, May 12, 2003.

_____. "Khatami Worried About Afghan Quagmire for U.S." *USA Today*, November 12, 2001. http://usatoday30.usatoday.com/news/attack/2001/11/12/khatami-usat.htm (accessed March 20, 2013).

_____. "Mutual Terror Accusations Halt U.S.-Iran Talks." *USA Today*, May 21, 2003. http://usatoday30.usatoday.com/news/world/2003-05-21-iran-usat_x.htm (accessed February 2, 2013).

_____. "Q&A with Iranian Foreign Minister Kamal Kharrazi." *USA Today*, September 18, 2002. http://usatoday30.usatoday.com/news/world/2002-09-18-iran-full-interview_x.htm (accessed March 1, 2013).

Sparrow, Bartholomew H. "Realism's Practitioner: Brent Scowcroft and the Making of the New World Order, 1989-1993." *Diplomatic History* 34, no. 1 (January 2010): 141-175.

Solomon, Jay, and David S. Cloud. "A Globe Journal Report: U.S.-Seoul Gap Feeds Korea Crisis." *Wall Street Journal*, January 2, 2003.

Tenet, George. *At the Center of the Storm: My Years at the CIA.* New York: Harper Collins, 2007.

Time Magazine Photo Essay. "Tehran Candlelight Vigil." (September 18, 2001). www.time.com/time/europe/photoessays/vigil/2.html (accessed December 1, 2012).

Timmerman, Kenneth R. "Fanning the Flames: Guns, Greed & Geopolitics in the Gulf War." The Iran Brief. www.iran.org/tib/krt/fanning_ch7.htm (accessed March 12, 2013).

University of California, Santa Barbara. The American Presidency Project, "Excerpts From the Tower Commission's Report." http://www.presidency.ucsb.edu/PS157/assignment%20files%20public/TOWER%20EXCERPTS.htm (accessed March 15, 2013).

UPI.com. "Perry: U.S. Eyed Iran Attack After Bombing." June 6, 2007. http://www.upi.com/Business_News/Security-Industry/2007/06/06/Perry-US-eyed-Iran-attack-after-bombing/UPI-70451181161509/ (accessed January 21, 2013).

U. S. Census Bureau. "Foreign Trade in Goods with Iran—1992." http://www.census.gov/foreign-trade/balance/c5070.html#1992 (accessed March 1, 2013).

_____. "Foreign Trade in Goods with Iran—1995." http://www.census.gov/foreign-trade/balance/c5070.html#1995 (accessed March 1, 2013).

U.S. Department of State. "Press Briefing on Board Plane En Route Moscow." Archive (2001-2009) (December 9, 2001). http://2001-2009.state.gov/secretary/former/powell/remarks/2001/dec/6759.htm (accessed March 1, 2013).

U.S. Department of State. Office of the Coordinator for Counterterrorism. "Executive Order 13224." (September 23, 2001). http://www.state.gov/j/ct/ris/other/des/122570.htm (accessed January 30, 2013).

_____. "Foreign Terrorist Organizations." (October 8, 1997). http://www.state.gov/www/global/terrorism/ terrorist_orgs_list.html (accessed March 20, 2013).

U.S. Congress. House. Committee on Government Oversight and Reform. "U.S. Diplomacy With Iran: The Limits of Tactical Engagement." Testimony of Hillary Mann before the Subcommittee on National Security and Foreign Affairs. 110th Cong., 1st sess., November 7, 2007. http://democrats.oversight.house.gov/images/stories/subcommittees/NS_Subcommittee/11.7.07_Iran_II/HillaryMannLeveretttestimony1107.pdf (accessed March 1, 2013).

U.S. Government Printing Office. Federal Register, vol. 60, no. 52, "Executive Order 12957 of March 15, 1995." http://www.gpo.gov/fdsys/pkg/FR-1995-03-17/pdf/95-6849.pdf (accessed February 10, 2013).

_____. Federal Register 60, no. 52, "Executive Order 12959 of May 6, 1995." http://www.gpo.gov/fdsys/pkg/FR-1995-05-09/pdf/95-11694.pdf (accessed February 10, 2013);

Usher, Evan. "A Series of Missed Opportunities—The Algiers Accords." *American Iranian Council News*, August 31, 2012. http://american-iranian.org/print/644 (accessed January 17, 2013).

Valinejad, Afshin. "Iran Says a U.S. Attack on it Would be an 'Irreparable Mistake.'" *Associated Press*, February 4, 2002.

Voice of America. "Iran Criticizes President Bush's Comments on Dissident Cleric." July 14, 2002. http://www.voanews.com/content/a-13-a-2002-07-14-6-iran-66500677/552934.html (accessed March 29, 2013).

Warrick, Joby, and Glenn Kessler. "Iran Had Secret Nuclear Program, U.N. Agency Says; 'No Evidence' of Arms Plans; Probe Continues." *Washington Post*, November 11, 2003.

Washington Post. "Text of President Bush's Address to a Joint Session of Congress and the Nation." September 20, 2011. http://www.washingtonpost.com/wpsrv/nation/specials/attacked/transcripts/bushaddress_092001.html (accessed January 29, 2013).

_____. "Text of President Bush's 2002 State of the Union Address." January 29, 2002. http://www.washingtonpost.com/wp-srv/onpolitics/transcripts/sou012902.htm (accessed January 30, 2013).

Well, Tim. *444 Days: The Hostages Remember*. San Diego: Harcourt Brace Jovanovich, 1985.

Weisman, Steven R. "Aftereffects: The Attack; Bush Condemns Saudi Blasts; 7 Americans are Dead." *New York Times*, May 14, 2003. http://www.nytimes.com/2003/05/14/world/aftereffects-the-attack-bush-condemns-saudi-blasts-7-americans-are-dead.html (accessed February 2, 2013).

Weisman, Steven R. "U.S. Demands That Iran Turn Over Qaeda Agents and Join Saudi Inquiry." *New York Times*, May 26, 2003.

Woodward, Bob. *State of Denial: Bush At War Part III*. London: Simon and Schuster, 2006.

Wright, Robin B. *In the Name of God: The Khomeini Decade*. New York: Simon and Schuster, 1989.

Wright, Robin B., ed. *The Iran Primer: Power, Politics, and U.S. Policy*. Washington, DC: United States Institute of Peace, 2010.